Anonymus

# List of William Blackwood and Sons' Publications

Anonymus

**List of William Blackwood and Sons' Publications**

ISBN/EAN: 9783742846488

Manufactured in Europe, USA, Canada, Australia, Japa

Cover: Foto ©Andreas Hilbeck / pixelio.de

Manufactured and distributed by brebook publishing software
(www.brebook.com)

Anonymus

**List of William Blackwood and Sons' Publications**

# LIST

OF

# WILLIAM BLACKWOOD & SONS'

# PUBLICATIONS

MDCCCLXXIV

45 GEORGE STREET, EDINBURGH

AND

37 PATERNOSTER ROW

LONDON

# CONTENTS.

# LIST OF BOOKS

PUBLISHED BY

## WILLIAM BLACKWOOD & SONS,

45 GEORGE STREET, EDINBURGH,

AND

37 PATERNOSTER ROW, LONDON.

--------◆--------

**Alison**—THE HISTORY OF EUROPE.
FROM THE COMMENCEMENT OF THE FRENCH REVOLUTION IN 1789 TO
THE BATTLE OF WATERLOO. By SIR ARCHIBALD ALISON, BART.,
D.C.L. Library Edition, 14 vols. demy 8vo, with Portraits and a copious
Index, £10, 10s.

On Large Paper, 14 vols., £14, 14s.
Crown 8vo Edition, 20 vols., £6.
PEOPLE'S EDITION, 12 vols., closely printed in double columns, £2, 8s. ;
and Index Volume, 3s.

"There is no book extant that treats so well of the period to the illustration of which Mr
Alison's labours have been devoted. It exhibits great knowledge, patient research, indefatigable
industry, and vast power."—*Times.*
"A valuable addition to European literature, evidently compiled with the utmost care, and its
narration, so far as we can judge, not perverted by the slightest partiality."—*Edinburgh Review.*
"One of the most important works which literature has produced. His sources of information
and authorities are of the richest and most comprehensive description. Though his opinions are
on the Conservative side, he allows every party to speak for itself, and unshake with a master's
hand how far institutions make nations great, and mighty, and prosperous."—*Preface to the German Translation.*

--------

—— CONTINUATION OF THE HISTORY OF EUROPE,
FROM THE FALL OF NAPOLEON TO THE ACCESSION OF LOUIS NAPOLEON.
By the SAME. Uniform with the Library Edition of the foregoing, 9 vols.,
£6, 7s. 6d.

PEOPLE'S EDITION, 8 vols. crown 8vo, 34s.

--------

These volumes—the History and Continuation—contain a continuous and systematic
account of Home and Foreign Events from 1774 to 1852, also Sketches of Art,
Literature, and Social Progress in the principal European States during that period,
which will nowhere else be found in the same limited space, with a full History of
Contemporary Events in British India.

--------

—— ATLAS TO ALISON'S HISTORY OF EUROPE;
Containing 109 Maps and Plans of Countries, Battles, Sieges, and Sea-
Fights. Constructed by A. KEITH JOHNSTON, F.R.S.E. With
Vocabulary of Military and Marine Terms. Library Edition, £3, 3s. ;
PEOPLE'S EDITION, £1, 11s. 6d.

**Alison**—EPITOME OF ALISON'S HISTORY OF EUROPE.
Seventeenth Edition, 7s. 6d., bound.

———— ATLAS TO EPITOME OF HISTORY OF EUROPE.
4to, 7s.

———— LIFE OF JOHN DUKE OF MARLBOROUGH.
With some Account of his Contemporaries, and of the War of the Succession.
By the Same. Third Edition, 2 vols. 8vo. Portraits and Maps, 30s.

———— ESSAYS: HISTORICAL, POLITICAL, AND MISCEL-
LANEOUS. By the Same. 3 vols. demy 8vo, 45s.

———— LIVES OF LORD CASTLEREAGH AND SIR
CHARLES STEWART, Second and Third Marquesses of London-
derry. From the Original Papers of the Family. By the Same. 3 vols.
8vo, £2, 2s.

———— THE PRINCIPLES OF POPULATION,
And their Connection with Human Happiness. By the Same.
2 vols. 8vo, 30s.

**Alison** — ON THE MANAGEMENT OF THE POOR IN
SCOTLAND, and its Effects on the Health of the Great Towns.
By WILLIAM PULTENEY ALISON, M.D. Crown 8vo, 5s. 6d.

**Aird**—POETICAL WORKS OF THOMAS AIRD.
Fourth Edition, fcap. 8vo, 6s.

———— THE OLD BACHELOR IN THE OLD SCOTTISH
VILLAGE. By the Same. Fcap. 8vo, 4s.

**Austin**—INTERLUDES.
By ALFRED AUSTIN. Fcap. 8vo, 5s.
THE MADONNA'S CHILD. By the Same. Crown 8vo, 7s. 6d.
ROME OR DEATH! By the Same. Crown 8vo, 9s.
THE GOLDEN AGE. By the Same. Fcap. 8vo, 6s.
THE SEASON; A Satire. By the Same. 5s.

**Aytoun**—LAYS OF THE SCOTTISH CAVALIERS, AND
OTHER POEMS. By W. EDMONDSTOUNE AYTOUN, D.C.L.,
Professor of Rhetoric and Belles-Lettres in the University of Edinburgh.
Twenty-second Edition. Fcap. 8vo, 7s. 6d.

"Mr Aytoun's 'Lays' are truly beautiful, and are perfect poems of their class, pregnant with fire,
with patriotic ardour, with loyal zeal, with exquisite pathos, with noble passion. Who can hear
the opening lines descriptive of Edinburgh after the great battle of Flodden, and not feel that the
minstrel's soul has caught the genuine inspiration?"—*Morning Post.*
"Professor Aytoun's 'Lays of the Scottish Cavaliers'—a volume of verse which shows that Scotland has yet a poet. Full of the true fire, it now stirs and swells like a trumpet-note—now sinks
in cadences sad and wild as the wail of a Highland dirge."—*Quarterly Review.*

**Aytoun**—LAYS OF THE SCOTTISH CAVALIERS.
An Illustrated Edition. From designs by SIR J. NOEL PATON and W. H. PATON, R.S.A. Engraved by John Thomson, W. J. Linton, W. Thomas, Whymper, Cooper, Green, Dalziel, Evans, &c. In small quarto, printed on toned paper, bound in gilt cloth, 21s.

"The artists have excelled themselves in the engravings which they have furnished. Seizing the spirit of Mr Aytoun's 'Ballads' as perhaps none but Scotchmen could have seized it, they have thrown their whole strength into the work with a heartiness which others would do well to imitate. Whoever there may be that does not know these 'Lays' we recommend at once to make their acquaintance in this edition, wherein author and artist illustrate each other as kindred spirits should."—*Standard.*

—— BOTHWELL : A POEM.
By the SAME. Third Edition. Fcap. 8vo, 7s. 6d.

"A noble poem, healthy in tone and purely English in language, and closely linked to the historical traditions of his native country."—*John Bull.*

"Professor Aytoun has produced a fine poem and an able argument, and 'Bothwell' will assuredly take its stand among the classics of Scottish Literature."—*The Press.*

—— THE BALLADS OF SCOTLAND.
Edited by the SAME. Fourth Edition. 2 vols. fcap. 8vo, 12s.

"No country can boast of a richer collection of Ballads than Scotland, and no Editor for these Ballads could be found more accomplished than Professor Aytoun. He has sent forth two beautiful volumes which range with Percy's 'Reliques'—which, for completeness and accuracy, have little to be desired—which must henceforth be considered as the standard edition of the Scottish Ballads, and which we commend as a model to any among ourselves who may think of doing like service to the English Ballads."—*The Times.*

—— FIRMILIAN, OR THE STUDENT OF BADAJOS.
A Spasmodic Tragedy. By T. PERCY JONES (by the Same). In small 8vo, 5s.

"Humour of a kind most rare at all times, and especially in the present day, runs through every page ; and passages of true poetry and delicious versification prevent the continual play of sarcasm from becoming tedious."—*Literary Gazette.*

—— NORMAN SINCLAIR.
By the SAME. 3 vols. post 8vo, 31s. 6d.

—— MEMOIR OF WILLIAM E. AYTOUN, D.C.L.
Author of 'Lays of the Scottish Cavaliers,' &c. By THEODORE MARTIN. With Portrait. Post 8vo, 12s.

**Ballantine**—LILIAS LEE, AND OTHER POEMS.
By JAMES BALLANTINE, Author of 'The Gaberlunzie's Wallet,' &c. Fcap. 8vo, 5s.

BATTLE OF DORKING. REMINISCENCES OF A VOLUNTEER : From 'Blackwood's Magazine.' Second Hundredth Thousand, 6d.

**Bethune**—TABLES FOR TRAVELLERS.
Adapted to the Pocket or Sextant-case. Compiled by ADMIRAL BETHUNE, C.B., F.R.A.S., and F.R.G.S. Cloth, 3s. 6d.

## Blackmore—THE MAID OF SKER.

By R. D. BLACKMORE, Author of 'Lorna Doone,' &c. Originally published in 'Blackwood's Magazine.' New Edition, crown 8vo, 7s. 6d.

"His descriptions are wonderfully vivid and natural, although he loves to paint nature in her most extravagant freaks. His pages are brightened everywhere with quiet humour, the quaint dry turns of thought remind you occasionally of Fielding."—*Times.*

## BLACKWOOD'S MAGAZINE.

FROM COMMENCEMENT IN 1817 TO DECEMBER 1873. Nos. 1 to 698, forming 114 volumes.

## INDEX TO BLACKWOOD'S MAGAZINE.

The First 50 Volumes. Octavo, 15s.

## TALES FROM "BLACKWOOD."

12 volumes. Sewed, 12s. Bound in cloth, 18s. The Volumes are sold separately, 1s. and 1s. 6d., and may be had of most Booksellers, in 6 volumes, handsomely half-bound in red morocco, 28s. 12 volumes in 6, half Roxburghe, 21s. 12 volumes, half-calf, richly gilt, 30s.

## BLACKWOOD'S STANDARD NOVELS.

Uniform in size and legibly printed. Each Novel complete in One Volume.

### Florin Series, Illustrated Boards.

TOM CRINGLE'S LOG. By Michael Scott.
CRUISE OF THE MIDGE. By the Author of 'Tom Cringle's Log.'
CYRIL THORNTON. By Captain Hamilton.
ANNALS OF THE PARISH. By John Galt.
THE PROVOST, AND OTHER TALES. By John Galt.
SIR ANDREW WYLIE. By John Galt.
THE ENTAIL. By John Galt.
REGINALD DALTON. By J. G. Lockhart.
PEN OWEN. By Dean Hook.
ADAM BLAIR. By J. G. Lockhart.
LADY LEE'S WIDOWHOOD. By Col. Hamley.
SALEM CHAPEL. By Mrs Oliphant.
THE PERPETUAL CURATE. By Mrs Oliphant.
MISS MARJORIBANKS. By Mrs Oliphant.

### Or in Cloth Boards, 2s. 6d.

### Shilling Series, Illustrated Cover.

THE RECTOR AND THE DOCTOR'S FAMILY. By Mrs Oliphant.
THE LIFE OF MANSIE WAUCH. By D. M. Moir.
PENINSULAR SCENES AND SKETCHES. By F. Hardman.
SIR FRIZZLE PUMPKIN, NIGHTS AT MESS, &c.
THE SUBALTERN.
LIFE IN THE FAR WEST. By G. F. Ruxton.
VALERIUS : A ROMAN STORY. By J. G. Lockhart.

### Or in Cloth Boards, 1s. 6d.

## BLACKWOOD'S MAPS OF THE COUNTIES OF SCOTLAND.

In Cloth Case for the Pocket, 1s. each.
The same strongly bound in leather, in one vol. post 8vo, 10s. 6d.

## Blagden—POEMS.

By the late ISA BLAGDEN. With a Memoir, by Alfred Austin. Fcap. 8vo, 5s.

**Bon Gaultier—THE BOOK OF BALLADS.**
Edited by BON GAULTIER. Eleventh Edition, with numerous Illustrations by Doyle, Leech, and Crowquill. Gilt edges, post 8vo, 8s. 6d.

**Hughes and Barham—THE BOSCOBEL TRACTS.**
RELATING TO THE ESCAPE OF CHARLES THE SECOND AFTER THE BATTLE OF WORCESTER, AND HIS SUBSEQUENT ADVENTURES. Edited by J. HUGHES, Esq., A.M. A NEW EDITION, with additional Notes and Illustrations, including Communications from the Rev. R. H. BARHAM, Author of the 'Ingoldsby Legends.' In Octavo, with Engravings, 16s.

"A very curious book, and about as good an example of single subject historical collections as may be found. Originally undertaken, or at least completed, at the suggestion of the late Bishop Copleston, in 1827, it was carried out with a degree of judgment and taste not always found in works of a similar character."—*Spectator.*

**Brackenbury and Huyshe—FANTI AND ASHANTI.**
THREE PAPERS ON ASHANTI AND THE PROTECTORATE OF THE GOLD COAST: WITH AN OUTLINE OF THE CAUSES THAT HAVE LED TO THE WAR. By CAPTAIN H. BRACKENBURY, Royal Artillery, Assistant Military Secretary to Major-General Sir Garnet Wolseley; and CAPTAIN HUYSHE, Rifle Brigade, Deputy-Assistant Quartermaster-General. Post 8vo, 5s. cloth.

**Brougham — MEMOIRS OF THE LIFE AND TIMES OF HENRY LORD BROUGHAM.** Written by HIMSELF. 3 vols. 8vo, £2, 8s. Each Volume sold separately.

**Bruce—FAMILY RECORDS OF THE BRUCES AND THE CUMYNS.** With an Historical Introduction and Appendix from Authentic Public and Private Documents. By M. E. CUMMING BRUCE. Quarto, cloth, £2, 10s. LARGE-PAPER EDITION, medium quarto, cloth, £3, 10s.

**Buchan—HANDY BOOK OF METEOROLOGY.**
By ALEXANDER BUCHAN, M.A., F.R.S.E., Secretary of the Scottish Meteorological Society, &c. A New Edition, being the third. [*In the Press.*]

In this Edition the Charts of the distribution of Atmospheric Pressure and of Terrestrial Temperature will be revised; the Relations of Temperature to Atmospheric Pressure and Winds will, with the aid of Illustrative Charts, be more fully discussed, and the principle will be applied in explanation of unusually Hot and Cold Seasons, as well as Seasons of excessive Drought or excessive Rainfall; Charts will be given showing the Distribution of Rain over the Continents of the Globe, and its connection with the Distribution of Atmospheric Pressure and Temperature, and with Prevailing Winds, will be pointed out; the Prevailing Winds over the Globe will be represented on Charts; and otherwise the book will be revised throughout.

—— INTRODUCTORY TEXT-BOOK OF METEOROLOGY.
By the SAME. Crown 8vo, with 8 Coloured Charts and other Engravings, pp. 218. 4s. 6d.

"A handy compendium of Meteorology by one of the most competent authorities on this branch of science."—*Petermann's Geographische Mittheilungen.*
"We can recommend it as a handy, clear, and scientific Introduction to the theory of Meteorology, written by a man who has evidently mastered his subject."—*Lancet.*
"An exceedingly useful volume."—*Athenæum.*

**Burke** — MEMOIR OF THE POLITICAL LIFE OF THE RIGHT HONOURABLE EDMUND BURKE, with Extracts from his Writings. By the REV. GEORGE CROLY, D.D. 2 vols. post 8vo, 18s.

**Burton**—THE HISTORY OF SCOTLAND:
FROM AGRICOLA'S INVASION TO THE EXTINCTION OF THE LAST JACOBITE INSURRECTION. By JOHN HILL BURTON, Historiographer - Royal for Scotland. New and Enlarged Edition. 8 vols. crown 8vo, with Index volume, £3, 3s.

"The best account that has yet been published of the national being and life of Scotland."— *Times.*
"Mr Burton has the highest qualifications for the task. In no other history of Scotland with which we are acquainted are there the especial attractive graces which distinguish those volumes of national history."—*Athenæum.*
"Mr Burton has given us, for its scale, one of the completest histories that we ever saw of any country."—*Saturday Review.*
"As a repository of the learning with which modern research and criticism have explored the national life of his countrymen, Mr Burton's history stands alone and without a parallel."—*British Quarterly Review.*

———— THE CAIRNGORM MOUNTAINS.
By the SAME. In crown 8vo, 3s. 6d.

" One of the most complete as well as most lively and intelligent bits of reading that the lover of works of travel has seen for many a day."—*Saturday Review.*

**Carlyle** — AUTOBIOGRAPHY OF THE REV. DR ALEXANDER CARLYLE, Minister of Inveresk. Containing Memorials of the Men and Events of his Time. Edited by JOHN HILL BURTON. In 8vo. Third Edition, with Portrait, 14s.

"This book contains by far the most vivid picture of Scottish life and manners that has been given to the public since the days of Sir Walter Scott. In bestowing upon it this high praise, we make no exception, not even in favour of Lord Cockburn's ' Memorials '—the book which resembles it most, and which ranks next to it in interest."—*Edinburgh Review.*

**Cave-Brown**—THE PUNJAB AND DELHI IN 1857:
BEING A NARRATIVE OF THE MEASURES BY WHICH THE PUNJAB WAS SAVED AND DELHI RECOVERED DURING THE INDIAN MUTINY. By the REV. J. CAVE-BROWN, Chaplain of the Punjab Movable Column. With Plans of the Chief Stations and of the different Engagements, and Portraits of Sir J. Lawrence, Bart., Sir H. Edwardes, Sir R. Montgomery, and Brig.-Gen. J. Nicholson. 2 vols. post 8vo, 21s.

" This is a work which will well repay the trouble of perusal. Written by one who was himself present at many of the scenes he narrates, and who has had free access to the papers of Sir J. Lawrence, Sir R. Montgomery, and Sir H. Edwardes, it comes with all the weight of official authority, and all the vividness of personal narrative."—*Press.*

CHRONICLES OF CARLINGFORD.
SALEM CHAPEL. 2s. in boards, or 2s. 6d. in cloth.
THE RECTOR, AND THE DOCTOR'S FAMILY. 1s. in boards, or 1s. 6d. in cloth.
THE PERPETUAL CURATE. 2s. in boards, or 2s. 6d. in cloth.
MISS MARJORIBANKS. 2s. in boards, or 2s. 6d. in cloth.

CAPTAIN CLUTTERBUCK'S CHAMPAGNE.
A WEST INDIAN REMINISCENCE. Post 8vo, 12s.

" We can conscientiously commend 'Captain Clutterbuck's Champagne' to all who like a really original story with no nonsense in it."—*Press.*

**Colquhoun—SPORTING DAYS.**
By JOHN COLQUHOUN, Author of the 'Moor and the Loch,' &c.
Crown 8vo, 5s.

——— **ROCKS AND RIVERS;**
OR, HIGHLAND WANDERINGS OVER CRAG AND CORREI, "FLOOD AND
FELL." By the SAME. 8vo, 6s. 6d.

——— **SALMON-CASTS AND STRAY SHOTS.**
Being Fly-leaves from the Note-Book of John Colquhoun, Esq. Second
Edition, fcap. 8vo, 5s.

——— **THE FERÆ NATURÆ OF THE BRITISH ISLES.**
By the SAME. 8vo, sewed, 1s. 6d.

——— **ON INSTINCT AND REASON.**
By the SAME. 8vo, sewed, 1s.

**COQUET-DALE FISHING SONGS.**
Now first collected by a North-Country Angler, with the Music of the Airs.
Octavo, 5s.

**Cotterill—PROEMS.**
THE ANGEL OF LIFE—SOLITUDE, &c. By H. B. COTTERILL. Fcap.
8vo, 4s. 6d.

**Courthope—THE PARADISE OF BIRDS:**
AN OLD EXTRAVAGANZA IN A MODERN DRESS. By WILLIAM JOHN
COURTHOPE, Author of 'Ludibria Lunæ.' Second Edition. 3s. 6d.

**Crawley—VENUS AND PSYCHE,**
WITH OTHER POEMS. By RICHARD CRAWLEY. Fcap. 8vo, 5s.

**Descartes**
ON THE METHOD OF RIGHTLY CONDUCTING THE REASON, AND SEEK-
ING TRUTH IN THE SCIENCES, AND HIS MEDITATIONS, AND SELECTIONS
FROM HIS PRINCIPLES OF PHILOSOPHY. In one vol. post 8vo, 4s. 6d.

**Dickson—JAPAN;**
Being a Sketch of the History, Government, and Officers of the Empire.
By WALTER DICKSON. 8vo, 15s.

"The entire work is not only pleasant and instructive reading, but one that ought to be read
and re-read by all who wish to attain anything like a coherent idea of the real condition of Japan.
Its value can hardly be overestimated."—*London and China Express.*
"Mr Dickson's work gives a general account of the History of Christianity in Japan more accurately than any preceding writer in the English language. . . . . His work is the most valuable
one that has yet appeared."—*Quarterly Review.*

**Dunbar—A FAMILY TOUR ROUND THE COASTS OF**
SPAIN AND PORTUGAL DURING THE WINTER OF 1860-61.
By LADY DUNBAR of Northfield. Post 8vo, 5s.

**Dwyer**—SEATS AND SADDLES, BITS AND BITTING, AND THE PREVENTION AND CURE OF RESTIVENESS IN HORSES. By FRANCIS DWYER. A New and Enlarged Edition. Crown 8vo, with Engravings, 7s. 6d.

**Eagles**—THE SKETCHER.
By the REV. JOHN EAGLES, A.M. Originally published in 'Blackwood's Magazine.' Octavo, 10s. 6d.

". . . . More instructive and suggestive readings for young artists, especially landscape-painters, can scarcely be found.—*The Globe.*

—— ESSAYS.
By the SAME. Originally published in 'Blackwood's Magazine.' Post 8vo, 10s. 6d.

CONTENTS :—Church Music, and other Parochials.—Medical Attendance, and other Parochials.—A Few Hours at Hampton Court.—Grandfathers and Grandchildren.—Sitting for a Portrait.—Are there not Great Boasters among us?—Temperance and Teetotal Societies.—Thackeray's Lectures : Swift.—The Crystal Palace.—Civilisation : the Census.—The Beggar's Legacy.

—— SONNETS.
By the SAME. Crown 8vo, 5s.

**Eliot**—MIDDLEMARCH: A STUDY OF ENGLISH PROVINCIAL LIFE. By GEORGE ELIOT. A New Edition. 4 vols. crown 8vo, 21s.

—— WORKS OF GEORGE ELIOT. LIBRARY EDITION.
ADAM BEDE. 2 vols. fcap. 8vo, 12s.
THE MILL ON THE FLOSS. 2 vols. fcap. 8vo, 12s.
SCENES OF CLERICAL LIFE. 2 vols. fcap. 8vo, 12s.
SILAS MARNER. Fcap. 8vo, 6s.
FELIX HOLT. 2 vols. fcap. 8vo, 12s.

—— WORKS OF GEORGE ELIOT. CHEAP EDITION.
ADAM BEDE. 3s. 6d.
THE MILL ON THE FLOSS. 3s. 6d.
SCENES OF CLERICAL LIFE. 3s.
SILAS MARNER. 2s. 6d.
FELIX HOLT. 3s. 6d.

—— THE SPANISH GYPSY.
By the SAME. Fourth Edition, crown 8vo, 7s. 6d.

" It is emphatically a great poem, great in conception, great in execution."—*Blackwood's Magazine.*
" She is a great writer, and in the 'Spanish Gypsy' she has achieved a great work."—*Times.*
" It is impossible, indeed, to speak too highly of the intellectual conception at the basis of the poem, and the finish and power with which it is worked out and adorned."—*Spectator.*

—— WISE, WITTY, AND TENDER SAYINGS,
In Prose and Verse. Selected from the Works of George Eliot. By ALEXANDER MAIN. Handsomely printed on toned paper, bound in gilt cloth. Second Edition, 6s.

" But undoubtedly George Eliot is the only woman of our time whose writings would be remembered for their humour alone, or whose sayings, just now collected into a volume by themselves, are at all likely, like Shakespeare's sayings, to pass into the substance of the language."—*Spectator.*

**Elder**—A MEMOIR OF JOHN ELDER.
Engineer and Shipbuilder. By W. J. MACQUORN RANKINE. With Portrait. Crown 8vo, 2s. 6d.

**Ewald**—THE CROWN AND ITS ADVISERS;
OR, QUEEN, MINISTERS, LORDS, AND COMMONS. By ALEXANDER CHARLES EWALD, F.S.A. Crown 8vo, 5s.

" . . . A commendable attempt to explain in simple and popular language the machinery of the English Government."—*Pall Mall Gazette.*
" May be regarded in some respects as a Constitutional Manual."—*Standard.*

**Finlay**—HISTORY OF GREECE UNDER FOREIGN DOMINATION. By GEORGE FINLAY, LL.D., Athens. 7 vols. 8vo, £3, 18s.

"His book is worthy to take its place among the remarkable works on Greek history which form one of the chief glories of English scholarship. The history of Greece is but half told without it."—*London Guardian.*
"His work is therefore learned and profound. It throws a flood of light upon an important though obscure portion of Grecian history. . . . In the essential requisites of fidelity, accuracy, and learning, Mr Finlay bears a favourable comparison with any historical writer of our day."—*North American Review.*

**Flint**—THE PHILOSOPHY OF HISTORY IN EUROPE.
Vol. I., containing the History of that Philosophy in France and Germany. By ROBERT FLINT, Professor of Moral Philosophy and Political Economy, University of St Andrews. [*In the Press.*

**Forbes**—THE CAMPAIGN OF GARIBALDI IN THE TWO SICILIES: A Personal Narrative. By CHARLES STUART FORBES, Commander, R.N. Post 8vo, with Portraits, 12s.

"A volume which contains the best sketch hitherto published of the campaign which put an end to Bourbon rule in the Two Sicilies. It is accompanied with plans of the chief battles; and its honest unexaggerated record contrasts very favourably with the strained and showy account of the Garibaldians just published by M. Dumas."—*Examiner.*

**Forsyth**—IDYLLS AND LYRICS.
By WILLIAM FORSYTH, Author of 'Kelavane,' &c. Crown 8vo, 5s.
"This is a little volume of unpretending but genuine poetry."—*Standard.*

FRENCH HOME LIFE.
By "an English Looker-on, who has lived for a quarter of a century in France amidst ties and affections which have made that country his second home."—*Preface.*
CONTENTS:—Servants.—Children.—Furniture.—Food.—Manners.—Language. —Dress.—Marriage. Second Edition, 6s.

"Nous en avons assez dit pour faire comprendre tout l'attrait que présente on pareil livre. En le lisant les Anglais apprendront à mieux nous juger; nous apprendrons, nous, à mieux nous connaître."—*Journal de Paris.*
"This is a work of singular knowledge, written by a man possessing rare powers of observation and social tact. That the writer has resided long in France, the most superficial glance into the book will make clear; for, whatever the passing traveller can do, he cannot attain to such result of clear picture, vivid contrast, and firm hold on general causes as we have here."—*British Quarterly Review.*
" 'French Home Life' is so rich in suggestive remarks and interesting details, it is so full of the knowledge derived from practical experience, that the reviewer is tempted, as the reader probably will be, to linger over its pages. A book like this is fruitful of thought and comment, and the kindly spirit that pervades it is worthy of all praise."—*Spectator.*
"A careful study of an interesting subject, exhibiting no little acuteness of observation and analytical subtlety. . . . He is not merely an entertaining, but a trustworthy, guide in the field of inquiry which he invites us to explore in his company."—*Saturday Review.*

**Forbes**—GEOLOGICAL AND PALÆONTOLOGICAL MAP OF THE BRITISH ISLANDS, including Tables of the Fossils of the different Epochs, &c. &c., from the Sketches and Notes of PROFESSOR EDWARD FORBES. With Illustrative and Explanatory Letterpress. 21s.

**Francillon**—EARL'S DENE. A NOVEL. By R. E. FRANCILLON. 3 vols. post 8vo, 31s. 6d.

**Galt**—THE NOVELS OF JOHN GALT.
ANNALS OF THE PARISH.
THE PROVOST.
SIR ANDREW WYLIE.
THE ENTAIL, OR THE LAIRDS OF GRIPPY.
    4 vols. fcap. 8vo, 2s. each.

**Gleig**—THE SUBALTERN.
By G. R. GLEIG, M.A., Chaplain-General of Her Majesty's Forces. Originally published in 'Blackwood's Magazine.' Library Edition. Revised and Corrected, with a New Preface. Crown 8vo, 7s. 6d.

**Goethe**—FAUST.
Translated into English Verse by THEODORE MARTIN. Second Edition, post 8vo, 6s.
    Cheap Edition, fcap. 8vo, 3s. 6d.
"The best translation of 'Faust' in verse we have yet had in England."—*Spectator.*

——— POEMS AND BALLADS OF GOETHE.
Translated by PROFESSOR AYTOUN and THEODORE MARTIN. Second Edition, fcap. 8vo, 6s.
"There is no doubt that these are the best translations of Goethe's marvellously-cut gems which have yet been published."—*The Times.*

**Grant**—A WALK ACROSS AFRICA.
OR, DOMESTIC SCENES FROM MY NILE JOURNAL. By JAMES AUGUSTUS GRANT, Captain H.M. Bengal Army, Fellow and Gold Medallist of the Royal Geographical Society. 8vo, with Map, 15s.
"Captain Grant's frank, manly, unadorned narrative."—*Daily News.*

**Grant**—MEMOIRS AND ADVENTURES OF SIR WILLIAM KIRKCALDY OF GRANGE, Governor of the Castle of Edinburgh for Mary Queen of Scots. By JAMES GRANT. Post 8vo, 10s. 6d.
"It is seldom, indeed, that we find history so written, in a style at once vigorous, perspicuous, and picturesque. The author's heart is thoroughly with his subject."—*Blackwood's Magazine.*

——— MEMOIRS AND ADVENTURES OF SIR JOHN HEPBURN, Marshal of France under Louis XIII., &c. By the SAME. Post 8vo, 8s.

——— MEMORIALS OF THE CASTLE OF EDINBURGH.
By the SAME. A New Edition. In crown 8vo, with 12 Engravings, 3s. 6d.
"Of the different books of this nature that have fallen in our way, we do not remember one that has equalled Mr Grant's 'Memorials of the Castle of Edinburgh.'"—*Spectator.*

**Grant**—INCIDENTS IN THE SEPOY WAR OF 1857-58.
Compiled from the Private Journals of GENERAL SIR HOPE GRANT, G.C.B. ; together with some Explanatory Chapters by CAPTAIN HENRY KNOLLYS, R.A., Author of 'From Sedan to Saarbruck.' Crown 8vo, with Map and Plans, 12s.

"His life during that period seems to have been one of half-stealth escapes, described, let us say at once, in a simple unaffected manner, as far removed from self-conscious bashfulness as from the swagger which even brave men sometimes exhibit, and which cannot but convey to the reader a very strong impression of the narrator's personal gallantry, and of his modest, straightforward, and kindly disposition."—*Saturday Review.*
"The book is delightful reading, and the stern interest of its subject is brightened by a pleasant style and a most fascinating variety of incidents."—*Pall Mall Gazette.*
"The journal which forms the bulk of the present volume was written day by day as the events happened, and written in a clear, unaffected style, lit up by a kindly, chivalrous spirit, which goes straight to the reader's heart. The story it unfolds is as full of incidents and adventures as any romance."—*Allen's Indian Mail.*

**Haig**—SYMBOLISM ;
OR, MIND, MATTER, AND LANGUAGE AS THE NECESSARY ELEMENTS OF THINKING AND REASONING. By JAMES HAIG, M.A. Crown 8vo, 12s.

"The book is in reality a popular exposition of philosophy and philosophical systems expressed in the clearest language. . . . The author occasionally displays considerable originality and ingenuity in his investigations. . . . He seems to suggest that philosophy and theology should go hand in hand. . . . Here we must take leave of this sturdy thinker with some admiration of his bold ideas and careful research. . . . The general reader will gather with little trouble from his pages some of the flowers of philosophical literature."—*Examiner.*

**Hamerton**—WENDERHOLME :
A STORY OF LANCASHIRE AND YORKSHIRE LIFE. By PHILIP GILBERT HAMERTON, Author of 'A Painter's Camp,' &c. 3 vols. post 8vo, £1, 11s. 6d.

**Hamilton**—LECTURES ON METAPHYSICS.
By SIR WILLIAM HAMILTON, BART., Professor of Logic and Metaphysics in the University of Edinburgh. Edited by the late Rev. H. L. MANSEL, B.D., LL.D., Dean of St Paul's ; and JOHN VEITCH, M.A., Professor of Logic and Rhetoric, Glasgow. Fifth Edition. 2 vols. 8vo, 24s.

———— LECTURES ON LOGIC.
By the SAME. Edited by Professors MANSEL and VEITCH. Third Edition. In 2 vols., 24s.

———— DISCUSSIONS ON PHILOSOPHY AND LITERATURE, EDUCATION AND UNIVERSITY REFORM. By the SAME. Third Edition. 8vo, 21s.

———— MEMOIR OF SIR WILLIAM HAMILTON, BART., Professor of Logic and Metaphysics in the University of Edinburgh. By PROFESSOR VEITCH of the University of Glasgow. 8vo, with Portrait, 18s.

"Professor Veitch has succeeded in blending the domestic with the intellectual life of Sir W. Hamilton in one graphic picture, as biographers rarely do succeed."—*Saturday Review.*

**Hamilton**—ANNALS OF THE PENINSULAR CAMPAIGNS.
By CAPTAIN THOMAS HAMILTON. A New Edition, Edited by F. HARDMAN. 8vo, 16s. Atlas of Maps to illustrate the Campaigns, 12s.

**Hamilton**—MEN AND MANNERS IN AMERICA.
By the SAME. With Portrait of the Author. Fcap., 7s. 6d.

**Hamley**—THE OPERATIONS OF WAR EXPLAINED AND
ILLUSTRATED. By EDWARD BRUCE HAMLEY, Colonel in the
Royal Artillery, Companion of the Bath, Commandant of the Staff College,
&c. Third Edition, 4to, with numerous Illustrations, 30s.

"We do not hesitate to say, the best treatise that has been written in the English language."—
*The Times.*

"On all matters relating to the practice of the profession, it forms the most perfect book of reference that has been published."—*United Service Magazine.*

——— THE STORY OF THE CAMPAIGN OF SEBASTOPOL.
Written in the Camp. By the SAME. With Illustrations drawn in Camp
by the Author. 8vo, 21s.

"We strongly recommend this 'Story of the Campaign' to all who would gain a just comprehension of this tremendous struggle. Of this we are perfectly sure, it is a book unlikely to be
ever superseded. Its truth is of that simple and startling character which is sure of an immortal
existence; nor is it paying the gallant author too high a compliment to class this masterpiece of
military history with the most precious of those classic records which have been bequeathed to
us by the great writers of antiquity who took part in the wars they have described."—*The Press.*

——— WELLINGTON'S CAREER;
A MILITARY AND POLITICAL SUMMARY. By the SAME. Crown 8vo, 2s.

——— LADY LEE'S WIDOWHOOD.
By the SAME. Crown 8vo, 2s. 6d.

"A quiet humour, an easy, graceful style, a deep, thorough, confident knowledge of human
nature in its better and more degrading aspects, a delicate and exquisite appreciation of womanly
character, an admirable facility of description, and great tact, are the qualities that command the
reader's interest and respect from beginning to end of 'Lady Lee's Widowhood.'"—*The Times.*

——— THE POSITION ON THE ALMA.
In Seven Sketches from the Field on the Day after the Battle. By the
SAME. Cloth, 5s.

——— OUR POOR RELATIONS:
A Philozoic Essay. By the SAME. With Illustrations, chiefly by Ernest
Griset. Crown 8vo, cloth gilt, 3s. 6d.

"A charming little book."—*Spectator.*

**Hamley**—A NEW SEA AND AN OLD LAND;
Being Papers suggested by a Visit to Egypt at the end of 1869. By
GENERAL W. G. HAMLEY. 8vo, with Coloured Illustrations, 10s. 6d.

"Such are the contrasts the book deals with, handling them in a style that is not only pleasant
but picturesque; and those who care to have ancient Egypt made easy will attain their object with
the smallest possible expenditure of temper and trouble by placing themselves under his guid-
ance."—*Saturday Review.*

HANDY BOOK OF LAWS
CHIEFLY AFFECTING SCOTLAND. Abridged and plainly stated for general
use. By an EX-SHERIFF-SUBSTITUTE. Sewed, 6d.

**HANDY HORSE-BOOK;**
OR, PRACTICAL INSTRUCTIONS IN RIDING, DRIVING, AND THE GENERAL CARE AND MANAGEMENT OF HORSES. By "MAGENTA." A New Edition, with 6 Engravings, 4s. 6d.

"As cavalry officer, hunting horseman, coach-proprietor, whip, and steeplechase-rider, the author has had long and various experience in the management of horses, and he now gives us the cream of his information."—*Athenæum.*
"He propounds no theories, but embodies in simple antechnical language what he has learned practically."—*Sporting Gazette.*

**Harbord—A GLOSSARY OF NAVIGATION.**
Containing the Definitions and Propositions of the Science, Explanation of Terms, and Description of Instruments. By the REV. J. B. HARBORD, M.A., Assistant Director of Education, Admiralty. Crown 8vo, illustrated with Diagrams, 6s.

—— **DEFINITIONS AND DIAGRAMS IN ASTRONOMY AND NAVIGATION.** By the SAME. 1s. 6d.

—— **SHORT SERMONS FOR HOSPITALS AND SICK SEAMEN.** By the SAME. Fcap. 8vo, cloth, 4s. 6d.

**Hardman—SCENES AND ADVENTURES IN CENTRAL AMERICA.** Edited by FREDERICK HARDMAN. Crown 8vo, 6s.

**Hastings—POEMS.**
By the LADY FLORA HASTINGS. Edited by her Sister, the late Marchioness of Bute. Second Edition, with a Portrait. Fcap., 7s. 6d.

**Hay—MYSIE'S PARDON.**
A NOVEL FROM AUSTRALIA. By JAMES WALKER HAY. 3 vols. crown 8vo, £1, 5s. 6d.

"The novel from Australia is clever and interesting, though it is probably more attractive to us through its facts than its fiction. The story is ably constructed, and all the characters are well sustained, while the author may fairly claim the credit of originality of design."—*Spectator.*
"'Mysie's Pardon' is an admirable picture of colonial human nature, which, in its social aspects, does not greatly differ from human nature at home. Mr Hay is a quick and intelligent observer; he has considerable literary tact and experience, and a keen sense of humour. . . . The book ends happily, and the reader will lay it down with regret at parting with so lively and entertaining a companion."—*Daily News.*
"The whole picture has a substance and a solidity about it which can hardly have been derived from any other source than fact. . . . It is not, however, merely as a colonial picture that 'Mysie's Pardon' is to be recommended. It is also a capital novel, both in plot and characters. Mysie herself is excellently drawn."—*Guardian.*

**Hay—A NOMENCLATURE OF COLOURS**
Applicable to the Arts and Natural Sciences, to Manufactures, and other purposes of General Utility. By D. R. HAY, F.R.S.E. 228 examples of Colours, Hues, Tints, and Shades. 8vo, £3, 3s.

—— **THE LAWS OF HARMONIOUS COLOURING.**
Adapted to Interior Decorations; with Observations on the Practice of House-Painting. By the SAME. Post 8vo, 6s. 6d.

—— **THE GEOMETRIC BEAUTY OF THE HUMAN FIGURE DEFINED.** To which is prefixed a System of Æsthetic Proportion. Applicable to Architecture and the other Formative Arts. By the SAME. 16 Plates. Royal 4to, 30s.

**Hay**—THE HARMONIC LAW OF NATURE
Applied to Architectural Design. By the SAME. 8 Plates. Royal 8vo, boards, 2s. 6d.

—— THE ORTHOGRAPHIC BEAUTY OF THE PARTHENON Referred to a Law of Nature. By the SAME. 12 Plates. Royal 8vo, sewed, 5s.

—— THE NATURAL PRINCIPLES OF BEAUTY,
As developed in the Human Figure. By the SAME. 5 Plates. Royal 8vo, sewed, 5s.

—— THE SCIENCE OF BEAUTY,
As developed in Nature, and applied in Art. By the SAME. 23 Plates. Royal 8vo, cloth, 10s. 6d.

—— THE NATURAL PRINCIPLES AND ANALOGY OF THE HARMONY OF FORM. By the SAME. 18 Plates and numerous Woodcuts. 4to, 15s.

—— PROPORTION;
Or, THE GEOMETRIC PRINCIPLE OF BEAUTY ANALYSED. By the SAME. 17 Plates and 38 Woodcuts. 4to, 25s.

—— ORIGINAL GEOMETRICAL DIAPER DESIGNS.
Accompanied by an Attempt to develop and elucidate the true Principles of Ornamental Design, as applied to the Decorative Arts. By the SAME. 57 Plates and numerous Woodcuts. Oblong folio, 4s.

—— THE PRINCIPLES OF BEAUTY IN COLOURING SYSTEMATISED. 14 Coloured Diagrams. Second Edition. By the SAME. 8vo, 15s.

—— FIRST PRINCIPLES OF SYMMETRICAL BEAUTY.
100 Plates. By the SAME. Post 8vo, 6s.

—— ON THE SCIENCE OF THOSE PROPORTIONS BY WHICH THE HUMAN HEAD AND COUNTENANCE, AS REPRESENTED IN ANCIENT GREEK ART, ARE DISTINGUISHED FROM THOSE OF ORDINARY NATURE. By the SAME. 25 Plates. Royal 4to, 36s.

**Hemans**—THE POEMS OF FELICIA HEMANS.
Complete in One Volume, Royal 8vo, with Portrait by Finden. Cheap Edition, 5s. The Same with Plates, gilt edges, extra binding, 7s. 6d. Another Edition, with Memoir by her Sister, Seven Volumes, fcap., 35s. Another Edition, in Six Volumes, cloth, gilt edges, 15s. The same 6 vols. bound in 3, 12s. 6d., or cloth extra, gilt edges, 15s.

The following Works of Mrs Hemans are sold separately, bound in cloth, gilt edges, 4s. each :—

| | |
|---|---|
| RECORDS OF WOMAN. | DRAMATIC WORKS. |
| FOREST SANCTUARY. | TALES AND HISTORIC SCENES. |
| SONGS OF THE AFFECTIONS. | MORAL AND RELIGIOUS POEMS. |

**Hemans**—SELECT POEMS OF MRS HEMANS.
In One Vol. fcap. 8vo, gilt edges, 3s.

——— MEMOIR OF MRS HEMANS.
By her SISTER. With a Portrait. Fcap. 8vo, 5s.

**Highland Society**—A DICTIONARY OF THE GAELIC LAN-
GUAGE. Comprising an ample Vocabulary of Gaelic Words, and Vocab-
ularies of Latin and English Words, with their translation into Gaelic;
to which is prefixed a Compendium of Gaelic Grammar. Compiled and
published under the Direction of the Highland Society of Scotland. 2
vols. 4to, cloth, £5, 5s.

**Homer**—THE ODYSSEY AND ILIAD.
Translated into English Verse in the Spenserian Stanza. By P. S. WORS-
LEY, M.A., Fellow of Corpus Christi College, Oxford; and JOHN CON-
INGTON, M.A., Corpus Professor of Latin in the University of Oxford.
4 vols. crown 8vo, 39s.

"If the translator has produced a book which, having caught the spirit of the poem, can delight
those to whom the original is a sealed book, he can desire no higher praise: and this praise belongs
justly to Mr Worsley. . . . He has placed in the hands of English readers a poem which
deserves to outlive the present generation."—*Edinburgh Review.*
"We assign it, without hesitation, the first place among existing English translations."—*Westminster Review.*

**Hosack**—MARY QUEEN OF SCOTS
AND HER ACCUSERS. By JOHN HOSACK, Barrister-at-Law. A New
and Enlarged Edition, 2 vols. 8vo, £1, 11s. 6d.

The Second Volume, containing a variety of Documents never before published, may be had separately, price 16s. 6d.

"A careful study of Mr Hosack's book will show that he has explicitly or implicitly answered
every one of the fifteen arguments in the famous Note L. of Hume's History of this reign."—
*Quarterly Review.*
"Whatever surmises may be formed about Mary's knowledge or assent, there can now be no
doubt that the murder was contrived, not by Mary, but by her accusers."—*Scotsman.*
"He has confuted those who, by brilliant writing and a judicious selection of evidence, paint
the Queen of Scots as an incarnate fiend, and who are dramatic poets rather than historians."—
*The Times.*

**Howell**—A CONCISE HISTORY OF ENGLAND TO THE
DEATH OF WILLIAM IV. By E. J. HOWELL. 8vo, 10s. 6d.

**Inglis**—BALLADS FROM THE GERMAN.
By HENRY INGLIS. Fcap. 8vo, 5s.

——— MARICAN, AND OTHER POEMS.
By the SAME. 8vo, 3s.

## Innes—THE LAW OF CREEDS IN SCOTLAND.

A Treatise on the Legal Relation of Churches in Scotland, Established and not Established, to their Doctrinal Confessions. By ALEXANDER TAYLOR INNES, M.A. 8vo, cloth, 15s.

"Most valuable and interesting book."—*The Edinburgh Review.*

"It must become the text-book of the subject among the members of the author's profession, as well as ecclesiastical reformers, statesmen, and politicians of all schools."—*The North British Review.*

"I cannot quote this work without expressing my strong admiration of its learning, ability, and (with a very few exceptions) impartial statement of the whole questions discussed in this address." —*Dean Stanley's "Address on the Connection of Church and State."*

## Johnson—THE SCOTS MUSICAL MUSEUM.

Consisting of upwards of Six Hundred Songs, with proper Bases for the Pianoforte. Originally published by JAMES JOHNSON; and now accompanied with Copious Notes and Illustrations of the Lyric Poetry and Music of Scotland, by the late WILLIAM STENHOUSE; with additional Notes and Illustrations, by DAVID LAING and C. K. SHARPE. 4 vols. 8vo, Roxburghe binding, £2, 12s. 6d.

"That valuable reservoir of Scottish song—the 'Scots Musical Museum.'"—*Notes and Queries.*

## Johnston—THE ROYAL ATLAS OF MODERN GEOGRAPHY.

In a Series of entirely Original and Authentic Maps. By A. KEITH JOHNSTON, F.R.S.E., F.R.G.S., Author of the 'Physical Atlas,' &c. With a complete Index of easy reference to each Map, comprising nearly 150,000 Places contained in this Atlas. A New Edition. Imperial folio, half-bound in russia or morocco, £5, 15s. 6d.; or with General Index in a separate volume, 8vo, both half-bound morocco, £6, 10s. Dedicated by special permission to Her Majesty.

"Of the many noble atlases prepared by Mr Johnston and published by Messrs Blackwood & Sons, this Royal Atlas will be the most useful to the public, and will deserve to be the most popular."—*Athenæum.*

"We know no series of maps which we can more warmly recommend. The accuracy, wherever we have attempted to put it to the test, is really astonishing."—*Saturday Review.*

"The culmination of all attempts to depict the face of the world appears in the Royal Atlas, than which it is impossible to conceive anything more perfect."—*Morning Herald.*

"This is, beyond question, the most splendid and luxurious, as well as the most useful and complete, of all existing Atlases."—*Guardian.*

"An almost daily reference to, and comparison of, it with others, since the publication of the first part some two years ago until now, enables us to say, without the slightest hesitation, that this is by far the most complete and authentic atlas that has yet been issued."—*Statesman.*

## —— THE HANDY ROYAL ATLAS.

45 Maps clearly printed and carefully coloured, with General Index. By the SAME. A New Edition. Imp. 4to, £2, 12s. 6d., half-bound morocco. Dedicated by permission to H.R.H. the Prince of Wales.

This work has been constructed for the purpose of placing in the hands of the public a useful and thoroughly accurate ATLAS of Maps of Modern Geography, in a convenient form, and at a moderate price. It is based on the 'ROYAL ATLAS,' by the same Author; and, in so far as the scale permits, it comprises many of the excellences which its prototype is acknowledged to possess. The aim has been to make the book strictly what its name implies, a HANDY ATLAS—a valuable substitute for the 'Royal,' where that is too bulky or too expensive to find a place, a needful auxiliary to the junior branches of families, and a *vade mecum* to the tutor and the pupil-teacher.

"This is Mr Keith Johnston's admirable Royal Atlas diminished in bulk and scale, so as to be, perhaps, fairly entitled to the name of 'Handy,' but still not so much diminished but what it constitutes an accurate and useful general Atlas for ordinary households."—*Spectator.*

"The 'Handy Atlas' is thoroughly deserving of its name. Not only does it contain the latest information, but its size and arrangement render it perfect as a book of reference."—*Standard.*

## Johnston—SCHOOL ATLASES.

ATLAS OF GENERAL AND DESCRIPTIVE GEOGRAPHY. By the SAME. A new and Enlarged Edition, suited to the best Text-Books ; with Geographical information brought up to the time of publication. 26 Maps, clearly and uniformly printed in Colours, with Index. Imperial 8vo, half-bound, 12s. 6d.

ATLAS OF PHYSICAL GEOGRAPHY, illustrating, in a Series of Original Designs, the Elementary Facts of Geology, Hydrography, Meteorology, and Natural History. By the SAME. A New and Enlarged Edition, containing 4 new Maps and Letterpress. 20 Coloured Maps. Imperial 8vo, half-bound, 12s. 6d.

ATLAS OF ASTRONOMY. By the SAME. A New and Enlarged Edition. 21 Coloured Plates. With an Elementary Survey of the Heavens, designed as an accompaniment to this Atlas by ROBERT GRANT, LL.D., &c., Professor of Astronomy and Director of the Observatory in the University of Glasgow. Imperial 8vo, half-bound, 12s. 6d.

ATLAS OF CLASSICAL GEOGRAPHY. By the SAME. A New and Enlarged Edition. Constructed from the best materials, and embodying the results of the most Recent Investigations, accompanied by a complete Index of Places, in which the proper quantities are given by T. HARVEY and E. WORSLEY, MM.A., Oxon. 21 Coloured Maps. Imperial 8vo, half-bound, 12s. 6d.

"This edition is so much enlarged and improved as to be virtually a new work, surpassing everything else of the kind extant, both in utility and beauty."—*Athenæum.*

ELEMENTARY ATLAS OF GENERAL AND DESCRIPTIVE GEOGRAPHY, for the Use of Junior Classes. By the SAME. Including a Map of Canaan and Palestine, with General Index. 8vo, half-bound, 5s.

"They are so superior to all School Atlases within our knowledge, as were the larger works of the same author in advance of those that preceded them."—*Educational Times.*
"Decidedly the best School Atlases we have ever seen."—*English Journal of Education.*
"The plan of these Atlases is admirable, and the excellence of the plan is rivalled by the beauty of the execution. . . . The best security for the accuracy and substantial value of a School Atlas is to have it from the hands of a man like our author, who has perfected his skill by the execution of much larger works, and gained a character which he will be careful not to jeopardise by attaching his name to anything that is crude, slovenly, or superficial."—*Scotsman.*

### —— INDEX GEOGRAPHICUS :

Being a List, Alphabetically arranged, of the Principal Places on the Globe, with the Countries and Subdivisions of the Countries in which they are situated, and their Latitudes and Longitudes. Compiled specially with reference to Keith Johnston's Royal Atlas, but applicable to all Modern Atlases and Maps. In 1 vol. imperial 8vo, pp. 676, 21s.

## Johnston—THE CHEMISTRY OF COMMON LIFE.

By PROFESSOR J. F. W. JOHNSTON. With 113 Illustrations on Wood, and a Copious Index. 2 vols. crown 8vo, 11s. 6d.

"It is just one of those books which will best serve to show men how minute is the providence which has been made for human support, and that if the laws prescribed by Nature are duly observed, she, on her part, will see to it that her functions are performed with fidelity and success."—*Durham Chronicle.*

### —— NOTES ON NORTH AMERICA :

Agricultural, Economical, and Social. By the SAME. 2 vols. post 8vo, 21s.

## Kinglake—THE INVASION OF THE CRIMEA :

Its Origin, and an account of its Progress down to the Death of Lord Raglan. By ALEXANDER WILLIAM KINGLAKE. Vols. I. and II., 32s., and Vols. III. and IV., 34s. Vol. V., Inkerman volume, *in the Press.*

**Lavergne**—THE RURAL ECONOMY OF ENGLAND, SCOT-
LAND, AND IRELAND. By LEONCE DE LAVERGNE. Trans-
lated from the French. With Notes by a Scottish Farmer. In 8vo, 12s.

"One of the best works on the philosophy of agriculture and of agricultural political economy
that has appeared."—*Spectator.*

**Lee**—LECTURES ON THE HISTORY OF THE CHURCH
OF SCOTLAND, FROM THE REFORMATION TO THE REVOLUTION
SETTLEMENT. By the late Very Rev. JOHN LEE, D.D., LL.D.,
Principal of the University of Edinburgh. With Notes and Appendices
from the Author's Papers. Edited by the Rev. WILLIAM LEE, D.D.
2 vols. 8vo, 21s.

**Lewes**—THE PHYSIOLOGY OF COMMON LIFE.
By GEORGE H. LEWES, Author of 'Sea-side Studies,' &c. Illustrated
with numerous Engravings. 2 vols., 12s.

CONTENTS :—Hunger and Thirst—Food and Drink—Digestion and Indiges-
tion—The Structure and Uses of the Blood—The Circulation—Respiration and
Suffocation—Why are we warm, and how we keep so—Feeling and Thinking—
The Mind and the Brain—Our Senses and Sensations—Sleep and Dreams—The
Qualities we inherit from our Parents—Life and Death.

LINDA TRESSEL.
By the Author of 'Nina Balatka.' 2 vols. fcap. 8vo, 12s.

**Lockhart**—DOUBLES AND QUITS.
By LAURENCE LOCKHART, late Captain 92d Highlanders. With
Twelve Illustrations. In 3 vols. post 8vo, 21s.

———— FAIR TO SEE.
A Novel. By the SAME. New Edition, in 1 vol. post 8vo, 6s.

"But politics are the smallest part of this very readable novel, the interest of which never flags,
for the story is as full of 'situations' as a good play."—*Times.*
" ' Fair to See' is something better than a clever novel. It shows no little artistic power; and
as you read it you feel that there is much more in the book than at first you fancied. . . .
The scenes on the moors, in the barracks, and the ball-rooms, are all dashed off by an expert.
These are minor merits, but they go far towards assuring the success of a story which marks a
decided advance on the author's first novel."—*Pall Mall Gazette.*

**Lyon**—HISTORY OF THE RISE AND PROGRESS OF
FREEMASONRY IN SCOTLAND. By DAVID MURRAY LYON,
one of the Grand Stewards of the Grand Lodge of Scotland; Honorary
Corresponding Member of the "Verein Deutscher Freemaurer," Leipzig,
&c., &c. In small quarto. Illustrated with numerous Portraits of Eminent
Members of the Craft, and Facsimiles of Ancient Charters and other curious
Documents. £1, 11s. 6d.

**Lytton**—THE PARISIANS.
By EDWARD BULWER, LORD LYTTON, Author of the 'Coming
Race,' &c. With Illustrations by SYDNEY HALL. 4 vols. crown 8vo,
26s.

**Lytton**—KENELM CHILLINGLY.
His Adventures and Opinions. By the SAME. 2 vols. fcap. 8vo, 10s.

—— WALPOLE; OR, EVERY MAN HAS HIS PRICE.
A Comedy in Rhyme. By the SAME. Fcap. 8vo, 5s.

—— LIBRARY EDITION OF LORD LYTTON'S NOVELS.
In Volumes of a convenient and handsome form. Printed from a large and
readable type. Fcap. 8vo, 5s. each volume.

THE CAXTON NOVELS:
The Caxton Family. 2 vols. | My Novel. 4 vols.

HISTORICAL ROMANCES:
Devereux. 2 vols. | The Siege of Grenada. 1 vol.
The Last Days of Pompeii. 2 vols. | The Last of the Barons. 2 vols.
Rienzi. 2 vols. | Harold. 2 vols.

ROMANCES:
The Pilgrims of the Rhine. 1 vol. | Zanoni. 2 vols.
Eugene Aram. 2 vols. | A Strange Story. 2 vols.

NOVELS OF LIFE AND MANNERS:
Pelham. 2 vols. | Ernest Maltravers—Second Part (i.e.
The Disowned. 2 vols. | Alice). 2 vols.
Paul Clifford. 2 vols. | Night and Morning. 2 vols.
Godolphin. 1 vol. | Lucretia. 2 vols.
Ernest Maltravers—First Part. | Kenelm Chillingly. 2 vols.
2 vols. |

"It is of the handiest of sizes; the paper is good; and the type, which seems to be new, is very
clear and beautiful. There are no pictures. The whole charm of the presentment of the volume
consists in its handiness, and the tempting clearness and beauty of the type, which almost con-
verts into a pleasure the mere act of following the printer's lines, and leaves the author's mind
free to exert its unobstructed force upon the reader."—*Examiner.*
"Nothing could be better as to size, type, paper, and general get-up."—*Athenæum.*

**Lytton**—FABLES IN SONG.
By ROBERT, LORD LYTTON, Author of 'Poems by Owen Meredith.'
Two vols. crown 8vo, 15s.

**M'Crie**—LIFE OF JOHN KNOX.
By the REV. THOMAS M'CRIE, D.D. Containing Illustrations of the
History of the Reformation in Scotland. Crown 8vo, 6s.
CHEAP EDITION, crown 8vo, 3s. 6d.

—— LIFE OF ANDREW MELVILLE.
Containing Illustrations of the Ecclesiastical and Literary History of Scotland in the Sixteenth and Seventeenth Centuries. By the SAME. Crown
8vo, 6s.

—— HISTORY OF THE PROGRESS AND SUPPRESSION
OF THE REFORMATION IN ITALY IN THE SIXTEENTH
CENTURY. By the SAME. Crown 8vo, 4s.

—— HISTORY OF THE PROGRESS AND SUPPRESSION
OF THE REFORMATION IN SPAIN IN THE SIXTEENTH
CENTURY. By the SAME. Crown 8vo, 3s. 6d.

**M'Crie**—SERMONS, AND REVIEW OF THE 'TALES OF MY LANDLORD.' By the SAME. In 1 vol. crown 8vo, 6s.

———— LECTURES ON THE BOOK OF ESTHER. By the SAME. Fcap. 8vo, 5s.

**Mackenzie**—STUDIES IN ROMAN LAW.
With Comparative Views of the Laws of France, England, and Scotland. By LORD MACKENZIE, one of the Judges of the Court of Session in Scotland. Second Edition, 8vo, 12s.

"We know not in the English language where else to look for a history of the Roman Law so clear, and at the same time so short. More improving reading, both for the general student and for the lawyer, we cannot well imagine ; and there are few, even among learned professional men, who will not gather some novel information from Lord Mackenzie's ample pages."—*London Review.*

"This is, in many respects, one of the most interesting works that the legal press has issued in our time. . . . The explanation of the Roman Law, historical and expository—the 'Studies' —is admirably given, clear and simple, and yet very learned, and the whole work is conceived in a candid and liberal spirit, being, besides, distinguished by a calmness of tone eminently befitting the judicial pen."—*Law Magazine and Review.*

**Manners**—GEMS OF GERMAN POETRY.
Translated by LADY JOHN MANNERS. Small 4to, 3s. 6d.

**Martin**—TRANSLATIONS BY THEODORE MARTIN :

GOETHE'S FAUST.
Second Edition, crown 8vo, 6s. Cheap Edition, 3s. 6d.

THE ODES OF HORACE.
By the SAME. With Life and Notes. Second Edition, post 8vo, 9s.

CATULLUS.
By the SAME. With Life and Notes. Post 8vo, 6s. 6d.

THE VITA NUOVA OF DANTE.
By the SAME. With an Introduction and Notes. Second Edition, crown 8vo, 5s.

ALADDIN :
A Dramatic Poem. By ADAM OEHLENSCHLAEGER. By the SAME. Fcap. 8vo, 5s.

CORREGGIO :
A Tragedy. By OEHLENSCHLAEGER. By the SAME. With Notes. Fcap. 8vo, 3s.

KING RENE'S DAUGHTER :
A Danish Lyrical Drama. By HENRIK HERTZ. By the SAME. Second Edition, fcap., 2s. 6d.

**Maurice**—THE SYSTEM OF FIELD MANŒUVRES
Best adapted for enabling our Troops to meet a Continental Army. Being the Wellington Prize Essay. By LIEUTENANT F. MAURICE, Royal Artillery, Instructor of Tactics and Organisation, Royal Military College, Sandhurst. Third Edition, crown 8vo, 5s.

"No work, English or foreign, has treated this subject (infantry tactics) better than the 'Wellington Prize Essay'"—*Times.*

"Lieutenant Maurice may well claim credit for having built up a work of such living interest as his is, even to the layman, upon such a set of dry bones as the given thesis afforded."—*Saturday Review.*

**MAXIMS OF SIR MORGAN O'DOCHERTY, BART.**
Originally published in 'Blackwood's Magazine.' Cloth, 1s.

**Mercer**—JOURNAL OF THE WATERLOO CAMPAIGN:
Kept throughout the Campaign of 1815. By GENERAL CAVALIE MER-
CER, Commanding the 9th Brigade Royal Artillery. 2 vols. post 8vo,
21s.

"No artist in the terrible scene . . . has ever painted it in more vivid colours than the
officer of artillery who led his troop into the very heart of the carnage, and resigned to write a book
more real, more lifelike, more enthralling, than any tale of war it has ever been our lot to read."—
*Athenæum.*

**Mitchell**—THE WEDDERBURNS AND THEIR WORK;
OR, THE SACRED POETRY OF THE SCOTTISH REFORMATION IN ITS HIS-
TORICAL RELATION TO THAT OF GERMANY. By ALEXANDER F.
MITCHELL, D.D., Professor of Hebrew, St Andrews. Small 4to, 2s. 6d.

**Mitchell**—BIOGRAPHIES OF EMINENT SOLDIERS OF
THE LAST FOUR CENTURIES. By MAJOR-GENERAL JOHN MIT-
CHELL, Author of 'Life of Wallenstein,' 'The Fall of Napoleon,' &c.
Edited, with a Memoir of the Author, by Leonhard Schmitz, LL.D.
8vo, 9s.

**Moir**—POETICAL WORKS OF D. M. MOIR (DELTA).
With Memoir by THOMAS AIRD, and Portrait. Second Edition. 2
vols. fcap. 8vo, 12s.

——— DOMESTIC VERSES.
By the SAME. New Edition, fcap. 8vo, cloth gilt, 4s. 6d.

——— LECTURES ON THE POETICAL LITERATURE
OF THE PAST HALF-CENTURY. By the SAME. Third Edition,
fcap. 8vo, 5s.

**Montalembert**—THE MONKS OF THE WEST.
From St Benedict to St Bernard. By COUNT MONTALEMBERT,
Member of the French Academy. 5 vols. 8vo, £2, 12s. 6d.

"Whatever the Count touches he of necessity adorns. He has produced a great and most interesting work, full of curious facts, and lit up with most noble eloquence."—*Times.*
"Of the translation we must say it is in every respect worthy the original. The nervous style
of the author is admirably preserved. It is at the same time spirited and faithful."—*Freeman's
Journal.*
"No library of English history will be complete without these glowing pictures of the 'Monks
of the West.'"—*Standard.*

——— MEMOIR OF COUNT DE MONTALEMBERT.
A Chapter of Recent French History. By Mrs OLIPHANT, Author of
the 'Life of Edward Irving,' &c. In 2 vols. crown 8vo, £1, 4s.

"Having a delightful subject, she has handled it in an altogether delightful way. . . . It is
as good, full, and truthful a portrait of his life and character as could be desired; and while the
skill of the author makes it as interesting as a novel, it may be read as an altogether trustworthy
chapter of recent French history."—*Examiner.*

**Murray**—CATALOGUE OF THE COLEOPTERA OF SCOT-
LAND. By ANDREW MURRAY of Conland, W.S., Member of the
Royal Physical Society of Edinburgh, of the Entomological Society of
France, &c. Fcap. 8vo, cloth limp, 2s. 6d.

**Neaves**—A GLANCE AT SOME OF THE PRINCIPLES OF
COMPARATIVE PHILOLOGY, as illustrated in the Latin and Angli-
can Forms of Speech. By the Hon. LORD NEAVES. Crown 8vo,
1s. 6d.

"Lord Neaves's remarks, as well as his very clear and well-ordered display of the principles of
the science, characterised by great modesty and simplicity, well deserve attention."—*Pall Mall
Gazette.*

——— THE USES OF LEISURE:
An Address delivered to the Students of the School of Arts, Edinburgh. By
the SAME, President of the School. Sewed, 6d.

——— ON FICTION AS A MEANS OF POPULAR TEACH-
ING. A Lecture. By the SAME. 6d.

NINA BALATKA;
The Story of a Maiden of Prague. In 2 vols. small 8vo, 10s. 6d., cloth.

**Nourse**—MODERN PRACTICAL COOKERY:
PASTRY, CONFECTIONERY, PICKLING AND PRESERVING, WITH A GREAT
VARIETY OF USEFUL RECEIPTS. By MRS NOURSE. Fcap. 8vo, boards,
5s. 6d.

**Oliphant**—PICCADILLY:
A Fragment of Contemporary Biography. By LAURENCE OLIPHANT.
With Eight Illustrations by Richard Doyle. 5th Edition, 4s. 6d.

"The picture of 'Good Society'—meaning thereby the society of men and women of wealth or
rank—contained in this book, constitutes its chief merit, and is remarkable for the point and
vigour of the author's style."—*Athenæum.*
"The real interest of 'Piccadilly' lies in the clever severeness with which it is literally jewelled.
They sparkle in every page. Mr Oliphant is one of the wittiest Jeremiahs of his time."—*Pall Mall
Gazette.*

THE SAME, WITHOUT ILLUSTRATIONS. 2s. 6d.

——— NARRATIVE OF LORD ELGIN'S MISSION TO
CHINA AND JAPAN. By the SAME, Private Secretary to Lord Elgin.
Illustrated with numerous Engravings in Chromo-Lithography, Maps, and
Engravings on Wood, from Original Drawings and Photographs. Second
Edition. In 2 vols, 8vo, 21s.

"The volumes in which Mr Oliphant has related these transactions will be read with the
strongest interest now, and deserve to retain a permanent place in the literary and historical annals
of our time."—*Edinburgh Review.*

——— RUSSIAN SHORES OF THE BLACK SEA IN THE
AUTUMN of 1852; with a Voyage down the Volga, and a Tour through the
country of the Don Cossacks. By the SAME. 8vo, with Map and other illustrations. Fourth Edition, 14s.

**Oliphant**—THE TRANSCAUCASIAN CAMPAIGN OF THE
TURKISH ARMY UNDER OMER PASHA: A Personal Narrative.
By LAURENCE OLIPHANT. With Maps and Illustrations. Post
8vo, 10s. 6d.

**Oliphant**—HISTORICAL SKETCHES OF THE REIGN OF
GEORGE SECOND. By Mrs OLIPHANT. Second Edition, in one
vol., 10s. 6d.

"Mrs Oliphant's Historical Sketches form two attractive volumes whose contents are happily
arranged so as to bring out some of the salient points at a period in our social history richly illustrated by epistolary and biographical remains."—*Examiner.*
"The most graphic and vigorous Historical Sketches which have ever been published. It is
indeed difficult to exaggerate the interest which attaches to these two volumes, or the high literary
merit by which they are marked."—*John Bull.*

——— CHRONICLES OF CARLINGFORD.
By the Same.

SALEM CHAPEL. 2s. in boards, or 2s. 6d. cloth.
THE PERPETUAL CURATE. 2s. in boards, or 2s. 6d. cloth.
MISS MARJORIBANKS. 2s. in boards, or 2s. 6d. cloth.
THE RECTOR AND THE DOCTOR'S FAMILY. 1s. sewed or 1s. 6d. cloth

——— JOHN: A LOVE STORY.
By the Same. 2 vols. post 8vo, 21s.

——— BROWNLOWS.
By the Same. 3 vols. post 8vo, 31s. 6d.

——— THE ATHELINGS:
Or, The Three Gifts. By the Same. 3 vols. post 8vo, 31s. 6d.

——— ZAIDEE: A ROMANCE.
By the Same. 3 vols. post 8vo, 31s. 6d.

——— KATIE STEWART: A TRUE STORY.
By the Same. Fcap. 8vo, with Frontispiece and Vignette, 4s.

**Osborn**—NARRATIVES OF VOYAGE AND ADVENTURE.
By REAR-ADMIRAL SHERARD OSBORN, C.B. 3 vols. crown 8vo,
12s., or separately:—

STRAY LEAVES FROM AN ARCTIC JOURNAL:
or, Eighteen Months in the Polar Regions in search of Sir John Franklin's
Expedition in 1850-51. To which is added the Career, Last Voyage, and
Fate of Captain Sir John Franklin. New Edition, crown 8vo, 3s. 6d.

THE DISCOVERY OF A NORTH-WEST PASSAGE BY H.M.S.
INVESTIGATOR, During the years 1850-51-52-53-54. Edited from
the Logs and Journals of Captain ROBERT C. M'CLURE. Fourth Edition,
crown 8vo, 3s. 6d.

QUEDAH; A CRUISE IN JAPANESE WATERS; and, THE FIGHT ON
THE PEIHO. New Edition, crown 8vo, 5s.

**Ossian**—THE POEMS OF OSSIAN

In the Original Gaelic. With a Literal Translation into English, and a Dissertation on the Authenticity of the Poems. By the REV. ARCHIBALD CLERK. 2 vols. imperial 8vo, £1, 11s. 6d.

"We feel assured that the present work, by the well condensed information it contains, by the honest translation of the Gaelic is given, by the new weight of its fair statements of fact, will do more to vindicate the authenticity of Ossian's Bard from the pompous ignorance of Johnson, the curious spite of Pinkerton, the cool incredulity of Laing, and even the self-asserting vanity of Macpherson, than any champion that has yet appeared."—*Glasgow Mail.*

OUR DOMESTICATED DOGS:

Their Treatment in Reference to Food, Diseases, Habits, Punishment, Accomplishments, &c. By the Author of the 'Handy Horse-Book.' 2s. 6d., bound in gilt cloth.

"How frequently do we hear ladies complain that just when their favourites come to know and love them, 'they are sure to die.' If instead of constantly cramming them with unwholesome food, they would follow the directions given in the pages before us, not only would the mortality be less, but the appearance and even the dispositions of their pets would be marvellously improved."—*Land and Water.*

**Outram**—THE CONQUEST OF SCINDE.

A Commentary. By GENERAL SIR JAMES OUTRAM, C.B. 8vo, 18s.

**Outram**—LYRICS, LEGAL AND MISCELLANEOUS.

By GEORGE OUTRAM, Esq., Advocate. Edited, with Introductory Notice, by HENRY GLASSFORD BELL, Esq., Advocate, Sheriff of Lanarkshire. Fcap. 8vo, 4s. 6d.

**Ovid**—THE METAMORPHOSES OF OVID.

Translated in English Blank Verse. By HENRY KING, M.A., Fellow of Wadham College, Oxford, and of the Inner Temple, Barrister-at-Law. Crown 8vo, 10s. 6d.

" An excellent translation."—*Athenæum.*
" The execution is admirable. . . . It is but sound and inadequate praise to say of it that it is the best translation of the Metamorphoses which we have."—*Observer.*

**Paget**—PARADOXES AND PUZZLES.

HISTORICAL, JUDICIAL, AND LITERARY. By JOHN PAGET, Barrister-at-Law. Octavo. 12s.

CONTENTS :—

THE NEW "EXAMEN;" or an Inquiry into the Evidence relating to certain Passages in Lord Macaulay's History concerning : I. The Duke of Marlborough. II. The Massacre of Glencoe. III. The Highlands of Scotland. IV. Viscount Dundee. V. William Penn. (Second Edition.)

VINDICATIONS.—I. Nelson and Caracciolo. II. Lady Hamilton. III. The Wigtown Martyrs. IV. Recollections of Lord Byron. V. Lord Byron and his Calumniators.

JUDICIAL PUZZLES.—I. Elizabeth Canning. II. The Campden Wonder. III. The Annesley Case. IV. Eliza Fenning. V. Spencer Cowper's Case.

ESSAYS ON ART.—Ruskin's Elements of Drawing. II. A Day at Antwerp : Rubens and Ruskin. III. George Cruikshank. IV. John Leech.

POEMS. By ISA.

Fcap. 8vo, cloth, 4s. 6d.

**Paton**—POEMS BY A PAINTER.
By Sir J. NOEL PATON. Fcap., cloth, 5s.

—— SPINDRIFT.
By the Same. Fcap., cloth, 5s.

**Patterson**—AN ESSAY ON THE NATIONAL CHARACTER OF THE ATHENIANS. By JOHN BROWN PATTERSON. Edited from the Author's revision by Professor PILLANS of the University of Edinburgh. With a Sketch of his Life. Crown 8vo, 4s. 6d.

**Patterson**—ESSAYS IN HISTORY AND ART.
By R. H. PATTERSON. 8vo, 12s.
CONTENTS :—Colour in Nature and Art.—Real and Ideal Beauty.—Sculpture.—Ethnology of Europe.—Utopias.—Our Indian Empire.—The National Life of China.—An Ideal Art-Congress.—Battle of the Styles.—Genius and Liberty.—Youth and Summer.—Records of the Past ; Nineveh and Babylon.—India : its Castes and Creeds.—"Christopher North"—in Memoriam.

"A volume which no discerning reader will open only once. Fine appreciative taste and original observation are found united with range of thought and rare command over the powers of the English language."—*Athenæum.*

—— THE SCIENCE OF FINANCE.
A Practical Treatise. By the Same. Crown 8vo, 14s.
CONTENTS :—
1. Our Invisible Capital : The Credit System.—2. Absorption of Specie.—3. International Trade : England and France.—4. The Balance of Trade.—5. What is Capital?—6. The Economy of Force.—7. The Potency of Capital.—8. Negotiability of Value : Commercial Currency ; Banking Currency ; Financial Currency.  9.—Fixed and Floating Capital.—10. Loanable Capital.—11. Banking Embarrassments.—12. The Rate of Interest.—13. Our Monetary System.—14. The Panic of 1866.—15. Impolicy of Bank Acts.—16. The Currency, Past and Present.—17. Foreign Systems of Banking.—18. The State and the Currency.—19. Monetary Reform.—20. Free Trade in Banking.—21. Reform of the Bank of England.—22. Banking Profits under the New System.—23. An International Monetary System.—24. Sunk Capital.—25. State Finance : Government Taxation and Expenditure ; the National Debt.—26. The State and the Railways.—27. Railway Finance : Defects and Remedies ; the Future of Railways.—28. Municipal Finance.—29. Land Finance.—30. The State, the Poor, and the Country.

—— THE ECONOMY OF CAPITAL ;
OR, GOLD AND TRADE. By the Same. 12s., cloth.
CONTENTS :—
I.—Thoughts on Gold.—II. What is Money?—III. The Golden Age. Effects of the Gold Discoveries on the World.—IV. The Economy of Capital. Banking. Financial Co-operation. Monetary Crises, 1793-1857.—V. The City of Gold.—VI. The Bank of England. Our Monetary System : Defects and Remedies.—VII. Our Trade. What is Over-Trading? Position of the London Joint-Stock Banks. Comparison of English and Scotch Banking, &c. &c.

"It displays throughout a thorough acquaintance with our Monetary System, and is written in the lucid and graceful style which distinguishes Mr Patterson's works."—*Morning Post.*
"A very brilliant chapter of Mr Patterson's volume is devoted to the City, and to the business carried on therein. . . . We feel almost as if we heard the roar of the ceaseless traffic, and joined in the restless activity, as we read Mr Patterson's descriptions."—*British Quarterly Review.*

**Pollok**—THE COURSE OF TIME; A POEM.
By ROBERT POLLOK, A.M. Small fcap. 8vo, cloth, gilt, 2s. 6d.
THE COTTAGE EDITION, 32mo, sewed, 1s. The Same, cloth, gilt edges,
1s. 6d. Another Edition, with Illustrations by Birket Foster and others,
fcap., gilt cloth, 3s. 6d., or with edges gilt, 4s.

———— AN ILLUSTRATED EDITION OF THE COURSE OF
TIME. The Illustrations by Birket Foster, Tenniel, and Clayton. In
large 8vo, bound in cloth, richly gilt, 21s.

"Of deep and hallowed impress, full of noble thoughts and graphic conceptions—the production
of a mind alive to the great relations of being, and the sublime simplicity of our religion."—
*Blackwood's Magazine.*

PORT ROYAL LOGIC.
Translated from the French ; with Introduction, Notes, and Appendix. By
THOMAS SPENCER BAYNES, LL.D., Professor in the University of
St Andrews ; Author of 'An Essay on the New Analytic of Logical Forms.'
Seventh Edition, 12mo, 4s.

"Through his excellent translation of the Port Royal, his Introduction and notes, Professor
Baynes has rendered good service to logical studies in this country ; for if the student desires to
understand something of the rationale of the rules laid down in ordinary texts, he could not have
recourse to a better work."—*London Quarterly Review.*

PUBLIC GENERAL STATUTES AFFECTING SCOTLAND.
Containing a Table of all the Public General Statutes, the Statutes affecting
Scotland being printed entire. With a General Index, and Tables of all the
General, Local, and Private Acts.

The Volumes are supplied at the following prices :— 11° & 12° VICTORIÆ, 1848,
8vo, cloth boards, 5s. ; 1849, 2s. 6d. ; 1850, 5s. 6d. ; 1851, 2s. 6d. ; 1852, 2s. 6d. ;
1853, 7s. ; 1854, 4s. 6d. ; 1855, 6s. ; 1856, 6s. 6d. ; 1857, 5s. 6d. ; 1858, 5s. ; 1859,
3s. 6d. ; 1860, 10s. ; 1861, 6s. ; 1862, 9s. 6d. ; 1863, 6s. ; 1864, 5s. ; 1865, 4s. ;
1866, 5s. ; 1867, 9s. ; 1868, 10s. 6d. ; 1869, with General Index to all the Public
Acts of Parliament relating to Scotland, 1800 to 1868, 9s. 6d. ; 1870, 8s. ; 1871, 8s. ;
1872, 9s. ; 1873, 6s. 6d.

PUBLIC SCHOOLS;
WINCHESTER — WESTMINSTER — SHREWSBURY — HARROW — RUGBY.
Notes of their History and Traditions. By the Author of 'Etoniana.'
Crown 8vo, 8s. 6d.

"In continuation of the delightful volume about Eton, we have here, by the same author, a volume
of gossip as delightful concerning five other public schools. Neither volume professes to be history,
but it is history of the best sort."—*Pall Mall Gazette.*

**Ramsay**—TWO LECTURES ON THE GENIUS OF HANDEL,
AND THE DISTINCTIVE CHARACTER OF HIS SACRED COMPOSITIONS.
Delivered to the Members of the Edinburgh Philosophical Institution.
By the Very Rev. DEAN RAMSAY, Author of 'Reminiscences of
Scottish Life and Character.' In crown 8vo, 3s. 6d.

**Reddie**—AN HISTORICAL VIEW OF THE LAW OF MARI-
TIME COMMERCE. By JAMES REDDIE, Esq., Advocate. 8vo,
14s.

**Ritter**—THE LIFE OF CARL RITTER,
Late Professor of Geography in the University of Berlin. By W. L.
GAGE. Crown 8vo, 7s. 6d.

**Rogers**—THE GEOLOGY OF PENNSYLVANIA:
A Government Survey; with a General View of the Geology of the United States, Essays on the Coal Formation and its Fossils, and a Description of the Coal-Fields of North America and Great Britain. By PROFESSOR HENRY DARWIN ROGERS, F.R.S., F.G.S., Professor of Natural History in the University of Glasgow. With Seven large Maps, and numerous Illustrations engraved on Copper and on Wood. In Three Volumes, Royal 4to, £8, 8s.

**Ross**—A VISIT TO THE CITIES AND CAMPS OF THE CONFEDERATE STATES. By FITZGERALD ROSS, Captain of Hussars in the Imperial Austrian Service. Crown 8vo, 7s. 6d.

**Rustow**—THE WAR FOR THE RHINE FRONTIER, 1870: Its Political and Military History. By COL. W. RUSTOW. Translated from the German by JOHN LAYLAND NEEDHAM, Lieutenant R.M. Artillery. Three vols. 8vo, with Maps and Plans, £1, 11s. 6d.

"The work is faithfully and intelligibly executed; and it is of importance that the work of one who was once himself a Prussian Officer, and who is confessedly one of the first military critics of the day, should be placed ready at hand for the perusal and consultation of that great mass of Englishmen who do not read German works in the original."—*Saturday Review.*

**Sandford and Townsend**—THE GREAT GOVERNING FAMILIES OF ENGLAND. By J. LANGTON SANDFORD and MEREDITH TOWNSEND. Two vols., 8vo, 15s., in extra binding, with richly-gilt cover.

"In the 'Great Governing Families of England' we have a really meritorious compilation. The spirit in which it is conceived, the care expended on the collection and arrangement of the material out of which the various memoirs are fashioned, and the vigorous and sometimes picturesque statement which relieves the drier narrative portions, place it high above the ordinary range of biographical reference books."—*Fortnightly Review.*

ST ANDREWS UNIVERSITY CALENDAR. Published yearly, price 1s. 6d.

**St Leonards**—LORD ST LEONARDS' HANDY BOOK ON PROPERTY LAW. Eighth Edition. Revised and enlarged, 5s.

"Seven large editions indicate the popularity which this admirable manual has obtained, not merely with the profession, but with the public. It should be made a text-book in schools. It gives just as much of the law as every man ought to know, conveyed in a manner which every man can understand. This new edition has been considerably enlarged by the venerable author."—*Law Times.*

ST STEPHENS;
Or, Illustrations of Parliamentary Oratory. A Poem. *Comprising*—Pym—Vane—Strafford—Halifax—Shaftesbury—St John—Sir R. Walpole—Chesterfield—Carteret—Chatham—Pitt—Fox—Burke—Sheridan—Wilberforce—Wyndham—Conway—Castlereagh—William Lamb (Lord Melbourne)—Tierney—Lord Grey—O'Connell—Plunkett—Shiel—Follett—Macaulay—Peel. Second Edition. Crown 8vo, 5s.

**Schlegel**—LECTURES ON THE HISTORY OF LITERATURE. Ancient and Modern. By FREDERICK SCHLEGEL. Translated by J. G. LOCKHART. Fcap., 6s.

A TREATISE UPON BREEDING, REARING, AND FEED-
ING, CHEVIOT AND BLACK-FACED SHEEP IN HIGH DIS-
TRICTS. By a LAMMERMOOR FARMER. Crown 8vo, cloth, 2s. 6d.

Shortrede—TRAVERSE TABLES TO FIVE PLACES,
FOR EVERY 2' OF ANGLE UP TO 100 OF DISTANCE. By ROBERT
SHORTREDE, F.R.A.S. Edited by EDWARD SANG, F.R.S.E.
8vo, 21s.

Simmons—LEGENDS, LYRICS, AND OTHER POEMS.
By B. SIMMONS. Fcap. 8vo, 7s. 6d.

Simpson—PARIS AFTER WATERLOO.
A Revised Edition of a 'Visit to Flanders and the Field of Waterloo.' By
JAMES SIMPSON, Advocate. With Two coloured Plans of the Battle.
Crown 8vo, 5s.

'Saturday Review'—SKETCHES AND ESSAYS.
Reprinted from the 'Saturday Review.'
CONTENTS :—Fashionable Scrambles in Country Houses.—The Return of the
Tourist.—The End of the Holidays.—Dinners in the Provinces, &c.—Weddings
and Wedding Presents.—Social Ladybirds.—The Infant's Progress.—Plato in
Petticoats.—Mohocks and their Literature.—Schools. In crown 8vo, 5s.

———ESSAYS ON SOCIAL SUBJECTS.
Originally published in the 'Saturday Review.' A New Edition. First and
Second Series. 2 vols. crown 8vo, 6s. each.

"Two remarkable volumes of occasional papers, far above the average of such miscellanies.
They are the production of a keen and kindly observer of men and manners, and they display a
subtle analysis of character, as well as a breadth of observation, which are remarkable. With
much of occasional force, these Essays have sufficient solidity to make a book ; and while they re-
call the wit of Montaigne and the playfulness of Addison, they are animated by a better moral
tone, and cover a larger range of experience."—*Christian Remembrancer.*

Smith—POEMS, SONGS, AND BALLADS.
By JAMES SMITH. Third Edition. 5s.

"The collection is certainly a rich and remarkable one, containing many specimens of finely
pathetic and descriptive verse, imbued with the true spirit of poetry and song."—*Scotsman.*
"A most meritorious and enjoyable volume."—*Courant.*

Smith—THORNDALE; OR, THE CONFLICT OF OPIN-
IONS. By WILLIAM SMITH. Second Edition. Crown 8vo, 10s. 6d.

"Mr Smith has read deeply and accurately into human nature, in all its weaknesses, fancies,
hopes, and fears. It is long since we have met with a more remarkable or worthy book.
. . . We know few works in which there may be found so many fine thoughts, light-bringing
illustrations, and happy turns of expression, to invite the reader's pencil."—*Fraser's Magazine.*

——— A DISCOURSE ON ETHICS OF THE SCHOOL OF
PALEY. By the SAME. 8vo, 4s.

——— DRAMAS,
By the SAME. 1. SIR WILLIAM CRICHTON. 2. ATHELWOLD.
GUIDONE. 24mo, boards, 3s.

SONGS AND VERSES:
    Social and Scientific. By an old Contributor to 'Maga.' A new Edition,
    with Music of some of the Songs. Fcap. 8vo, 3s. 6d.

"The productions thrown off by this eccentric muse have all the merits of originality and
variety. . . . He has written songs, not essays—such a hotch-potch of science and humour,
jest and literature, gossip and criticism, as might have been served at the Noctes Ambrosianæ in
the blue parlour at Ambrose's."—*Saturday Review.*

**Southey**—POETICAL WORKS OF CAROLINE BOWLES
    SOUTHEY. Fcap. 8vo, 5s.

"In one of these well-bound, neatly-printed, tonal paper editions, in turning out which our
leading publishers so laudably vie with each other, Messrs. Blackwood have gathered up the precious remains of Caroline Bowles Southey. We call them precious advisedly, because they illustrate a style of authorship which is somewhat out of date, and has been superseded by other
styles neither so natural nor so attractive to cultivated tastes. Caroline Bowles was nurard, so
to speak, in the school of nature, taught with all the fostering care of home influence, and allowed
to ripen in intellect and fancy amidst the varied charms of a country life."—*The Churchman.*

"We do not remember any recent author whose poetry is so essentially native; and this English complexion constitutes one of its characteristic charms. No purer model of our genuine home
feeling and language."—*Quarterly Review.*

———— THE BIRTHDAY, AND OTHER POEMS.
    By the SAME. Second Edition. 3s.

———— CHAPTERS ON CHURCHYARDS.
    By the SAME. Second Edition. Fcap. 8vo, 2s. 6d.

———— ROBIN HOOD; A FRAGMENT.
    By the late ROBERT SOUTHEY and CAROLINE SOUTHEY. With
    other Fragments and Poems. Post 8vo, 8s.

**Speke**—JOURNAL OF THE DISCOVERY OF THE SOURCE
    OF THE NILE. By J. H. SPEKE, Captain H.M. Indian Army. 8vo,
    21s. With a Map of Eastern Equatorial Africa by Captain Speke ; numer-
    ous Illustrations, chiefly from drawings by Captain Grant ; and Portraits en-
    graved on Steel, of Captains Speke and Grant.

"A monument of perseverance, courage, and temper displayed under difficulties which have
perhaps never been equalled."—*Time.*

"It is, however, a great story that is thus plainly told ; a story of which nearly all the interest
lies in the strange facts related, and, more than all, in the crowning fact that it forms as in a large
degree from a geographical puzzle, which had excited the curiosity of mankind—of the most illustrious emperors and commonalties—from very early times."—*Athenæum.*

———— WHAT LED TO THE DISCOVERY OF THE NILE
    SOURCE. By the SAME. 8vo, with Maps, &c., 14s.

**Sophocles**—THREE PLAYS OF SOPHOCLES : ANTIGONE,
    ELECTRA, AND DEIANIRA. Translated into English Verse by LEWIS
    CAMPBELL, M.A., Professor of Greek in the University of St Andrews.
    8vo, 6s.

———— THE KING ŒDIPUS AND PHILOCTETES OF SO-
    PHOCLES. Translated into English Verse by the SAME. 8vo, 5s.

**Stewart**—ADVICE TO PURCHASERS OF HORSES.
By JOHN STEWART, V.S. Author of 'Stable Economy.' 2s. 6d. To
the farmer, the sportsman, and all interested in obtaining a sound and well-
conditioned animal, calculated either for work or pleasure, this work will be
found to be eminently useful. It is the result of the experience of a first-
rate authority on the subject.

——— STABLE ECONOMY.
A Treatise on the Management of Horses in relation to Stabling, Grooming,
Feeding, Watering, and Working. By the SAME. Seventh Edition, fcap.
8vo, 6s. 6d.

**Story**—GRAFFITI D'ITALIA.
By W. W. STORY, Author of 'Roba di Roma.' Fcap. 8vo, 7s. 6d.

"As a sculptor's sketches in a kind of poetic neutral tint, they are of great value, quite apart
from their intrinsic value as poems."—*Athenæum.*
"In the present volume he has translated the marble for us into poetry. Goethe used to say that
sculpture was the most poetical of all the arts. And in a certain high transcendental sense he is
perfectly right. Those who are interested in the question should certainly study the Cleopatra of
Story in marble, and the Cleopatra, as we find her translated in the present volume into verse."—
*Westminster Review.*

STELLA AND OTHER POEMS.
By FLORENZ. Fcap. 8vo, cloth, 4s.

**Stirling**—THE PRIORY OF INCHMAHOME:
NOTES, HISTORICAL AND DESCRIPTIVE. By the REV. MACGREGOR
STIRLING. With an Appendix of Original Papers. Engravings. 4to,
31s. 6d.

**Strickland**—LIVES OF THE QUEENS OF SCOTLAND,
AND ENGLISH PRINCESSES CONNECTED WITH THE REGAL SUCCESSION OF
GREAT BRITAIN. By AGNES STRICKLAND. With Portraits and
Historical Vignettes. 8 vols. post 8vo, £4, 4s.

"Every step in Scotland is historical; the shades of the dead arise on every side; the very
rocks breathe. Miss Strickland's talents as a writer, and turn of mind as an individual, in a
peculiar manner fit her for painting a historical gallery of the most illustrious or dignified female
characters in that land of chivalry and song."—*Blackwood's Magazine.*

**Stuart**—LAYS OF THE DEER FOREST.
With Sketches of Olden and Modern Deer Hunting, &c. By JOHN
SOBIESKI and CHARLES EDWARD STUART. 2 vols. post 8vo, 21s.

**Swainson**—A HANDBOOK OF WEATHER FOLK-LORE:
Being a Collection of Proverbial Sayings in Various Languages relating to
the Weather, with Explanatory and Illustrative Notes. By the REV. C.
SWAINSON, M.A., Vicar of High Hurst Wood. Fcap. 8vo, Roxburghe
binding, 6s. 6d.

"The Rev. C. Swainson has compiled a work on weather-lore such as we have long desired to
see. He has performed his work well. Like all good work, it has evidently been a labour of love.
Mr Swainson brings many qualifications for his task. He is a scholar, and possesses the tastes of
a scholar. He does not confine himself to the weather-lore of England. He flings a wide net: he
has gathered from the best sources. He has laid the principal European works on the subject under
contribution. The result is a book which ought to find a place in every library."—*Westminster Review.*
"Enough has been said to illustrate the wealth of the store which Mr Swainson has opened in the
first part of his volume. The second part is not a whit less rich and interesting."—*Saturday Review.*
"Mr Swainson has produced a very curious and interesting book."—*Standard.*

**Swayne—LAKE VICTORIA.**
A Narrative of Explorations in Search of the Source of the Nile. Compiled from the Memoirs of Captains Speke and Grant. By GEORGE C. SWAYNE, M.A., Late Fellow of Corpus Christi College, Oxford. Illustrated with Woodcuts and Map. Crown 8vo, 7s. 6d.

"Mr Swayne has admirably discharged his task, and has produced a very excellent and truly readable volume."—*Daily News.*
"The volume before us is a very readable one. We anticipate for it a wide popularity."—*London Review.*

**Taylor—TARA: A MAHRATTA TALE.**
By CAPTAIN MEADOWS TAYLOR. 3 vols. post 8vo, 7s. 6d.

"A picture of Indian life which it is impossible not to admire. We have no hesitation in saying, that a more perfect knowledge of India is to be acquired from an attentive perusal and study of this work, than could be gleaned from a whole library."—*Press.*

—— **RALPH DARNELL. A NOVEL.**
By the SAME. 3 vols. post 8vo, 7s. 6d.

**Thomson—INTRODUCTION TO METEOROLOGY.**
By DAVID. P. THOMSON, M.D. Octavo, with Engravings, 14s.

**Tibullus—THE ELEGIES OF ALBIUS TIBULLUS.**
Translated into English Verse, with Life of the Poet, and Illustrative Notes. By JAMES CRANSTOUN, B.A., Author of a Translation of 'Catullus.' In crown 8vo, 6s. 6d.

"We may congratulate Mr Cranstoun on having occupied a place for which his poetical skill, no less than his manifest classical training and acquirements, abundantly fits him."—*Saturday Review.*
"He comes nearer the originals than any of his predecessors that we are acquainted with. . . . The notes are scholarly and really illustrative."—*Examiner.*
"By far the best of the few versions we have of this sweet and graceful poet."—*Standard*

**TOM CRINGLE'S LOG.**
A New Edition, with Illustrations. Crown 8vo, 6s.

"Everybody who has failed to read 'Tom Cringle's Log' should do so at once. The 'Quarterly Review' went so far as to say that the papers composing it, when it first appeared in 'Blackwood,' were the most brilliant series of the time, and that time ever unrivalled for the number of famous magazinists existing in it. Coleridge says in his 'Table Talk' that the Log is most excellent: and these verdicts have been ratified by generations of men and boys, and by the metropolitan of Continental approval, which is shown by repeated translations. The engravings illustrating the present issue are excellent."—*Standard.*

**Train—THE BUCHANITES FROM FIRST TO LAST.**
By JOSEPH TRAIN. Fcap. 8vo, 4s.

**A TRUE REFORMER.**
3 vols. crown 8vo, £1, 5s. 6d. Originally published in 'Blackwood's Magazine.'

**TRANSACTIONS OF THE HIGHLAND AND AGRI-CULTURAL SOCIETY OF SCOTLAND.** 1866-1871, 6 Nos., sewed, 4s. each; 1872-3-4, cloth, 5s. each. Continued annually.

**Tytler—THE WONDER SEEKER,**
OR THE HISTORY OF CHARLES DOUGLAS. By M. FRASER TYTLER. Author of 'Tales of the Great and Brave,' &c. A New Edition. Fcap., 3s. 6d.

**Van de Velde**—NARRATIVE OF A JOURNEY THROUGH SYRIA AND PALESTINE. By LIEUT. VAN DE VELDE. 2 vols. 8vo, with Maps, &c., £1, 10s.

**Virgil**—THE ÆNEID OF VIRGIL. Translated in English Blank Verse by G. K. RICKARDS, M.A., and LORD RAVENSWORTH. 2 vols. fcap. 8vo, 10s.

"Mr Rickards has done good service to the non-classical public by the faithful and beautiful version of Virgil's Æneid now before us, and he has enhanced the boon by a preface of special value, as setting forth fairly and considerately the respective merits of previous translations, and the special qualities of Virgil as a poet."—*Standard.*

"Lord Ravensworth's success and strength are to be found, not so much in his verbal force as in the Virgilian spirit which breathes throughout his lines. No English reader can well miss their poetical grace and vigour; no scholar will deem unfaithful the clean cut, decisive lines of this masterly version."—*Evening Standard.*

**Von Borcke**—MEMOIRS OF THE CONFEDERATE WAR FOR INDEPENDENCE. By HEROS VON BORCKE, lately Chief of Staff to General J. E. B. Stuart. 2 vols. post 8vo, with Map, 21s.

**Warren**—WORKS OF SAMUEL WARREN, D.C.L.
DIARY OF A LATE PHYSICIAN. In 2 vols. fcap., 12s. Another Edition, with Engravings, in crown 8vo, handsomely printed, 7s. 6d.
TEN THOUSAND A-YEAR. Three vols. fcap., 18s.
NOW AND THEN. Fcap., 6s.
MISCELLANIES. 2 vols. crown 8vo, 24s.
THE LILY AND THE BEE. Fcap., 8vo, 5s.

——— SAMUEL WARREN'S WORKS.
People's Edition, 4 vols. crown 8vo, cloth, 18s. Or separately :—
DIARY OF A LATE PHYSICIAN. 3s. 6d.
TEN THOUSAND A-YEAR. 5s.
NOW AND THEN. LILY AND BEE. INTELLECTUAL AND MORAL DEVELOPMENT OF THE PRESENT AGE. 1 vol., 4s. 6d.
ESSAYS, CRITICAL, IMAGINATIVE, AND JURIDICAL. 1 vol., 5s.

**ESSAYS WRITTEN FOR THE WELLINGTON PRIZE.** Selected for Publication, by His Grace's desire, from those specially mentioned by the Arbiter. 8vo, 12s. 6d.

*List of Authors.*

I. By Lieut. J. T. HILDYARD, 71st Highland Light Infantry.
II. By Lieutenant STANIER WALLER, Royal Engineers.
III. By Captain J. C. RUSSELL, 10th Royal Hussars.
IV. By Colonel Sir GARNET J. WOLSELEY, C.B., K.C.M.G.
V. By General J. R. CRAUFURD.
VI. By Lieutenant C. COOPER KING, Royal Marine Artillery.

**White**—ARCHÆOLOGICAL SKETCHES IN SCOTLAND—KINTYRE. By CAPTAIN T. P. WHITE, R.E., &c., of the Ordnance Survey. With 138 Illustrations. Folio, £2, 2s.

**WHY WOMEN CANNOT BE TURNED INTO MEN.** Price 6d.

**Wilson**—THE "EVER-VICTORIOUS ARMY."
A History of the Chinese Campaign under Lieut.-Col. C. G. Gordon, and of the Suppression of the Tai-ping Rebellion. By ANDREW WILSON, F.A.S.L., Author of 'England's Policy in China;' and formerly Editor of the 'China Mail.' In 8vo, with Maps, 15s.

"In addition to a good deal of information respecting China and its recent history, this volume contains an interesting account of a brilliant passage in the military career of an English officer of remarkable promise, and of the important results of his skill and heroism. . . . It brings out clearly the eminent qualities of Colonel Gordon, his intrepidity and resources as a military leader, his rare aptitude for a difficult command, his dauntless courage, calmness, and prudence, his lofty character and unsullied honour."—*Times.*

**Wilson**—WORKS OF PROFESSOR WILSON.
Edited by his Son-in-law, Professor FERRIER. In 12 vols. crown 8vo, £2, 8s.

——— THE NOCTES AMBROSIANÆ.
By the SAME. With Notes and a Glossary. In four vols. crown 8vo, 16s.

——— RECREATIONS OF CHRISTOPHER NORTH.
By the SAME. In two vols. New Edition, with Portrait, 8s.

"Welcome, right welcome, Christopher North; we cordially greet thee in thy new dress, thou genial and hearty old man, whose 'Ambrosian nights' have so often in imagination transported us from solitude to the social circle, and whose vivid pictures of flood and fell, of loch and glen, have carried us in thought from the smoke, din, and pent-up opulence of London, to the rushing stream or tranquil tarn of those mountain ranges," &c.—*Times.*

——— ESSAYS, CRITICAL AND IMAGINATIVE.
By the SAME. Four vols. crown 8vo, 16s.

——— TALES.
By the SAME. Comprising 'The Lights and Shadows of Scottish Life;' 'The Trials of Margaret Lyndsay;' and 'The Foresters.' In one vol. crown 8vo, 4s., cloth. Cheap Edition. Fcap. 8vo, 2s. 6d.

——— POEMS.
Containing the "Isle of Palms," the "City of the Plague," "Unimore," and other Poems. By the SAME. Complete Edition. Crown 8vo, 4s.

——— HOMER AND HIS TRANSLATORS, AND THE GREEK DRAMA. By the SAME. Crown 8vo, 4s.

**Wills**—CHARLES THE FIRST.
An Historical Tragedy in Four Acts. By W. G. WILLS, Author of 'The Man o' Airlie,' 'Medea,' &c. 8vo, 7s. 6d.

——— DRAWING-ROOM DRAMAS FOR CHILDREN.
By the SAME, and the Hon. Mrs Greene. Crown 8vo, 6s.

C

Wingate—POEMS AND SONGS.
By DAVID WINGATE.  In fcap. 8vo, 5s.

"Genuine poetic ore, poems which win for their author a place among Scotland's true sons of song, and such as any man in any country might rejoice to have written."—*London Review.*

—— ANNIE WEIR, AND OTHER POEMS.
By the SAME.  Fcap. 8vo, 5s.

Yule—FORTIFICATION ;
For the use of Officers in the Army, and Readers of Military History.  By Colonel H. YULE, Bengal Engineers.  8vo, with numerous Illustrations, 10s. 6d.

"An excellent manual : one of the best works of its class."—*British Army Despatch.*

---

## BOOKS IN THE PRESS:

---

MR KINGLAKE'S
FIFTH, OR "INKERMAN VOLUME" OF
## THE INVASION OF THE CRIMEA.

THE
## PHILOSOPHY OF HISTORY IN EUROPE.

VOL. I., CONTAINING THE HISTORY OF THAT PHILOSOPHY IN FRANCE AND GERMANY.

BY ROBERT FLINT,
Professor of Moral Philosophy and Political Economy, University of St Andrews.

## ECONOMIC GEOLOGY;
OR,
GEOLOGY IN ITS RELATIONS TO THE ARTS AND MANUFACTURES.

BY DAVID PAGE, LL.D., F.G.S., &c.
Professor of Geology in the Durham University College of Physical Science, Newcastle.

## ARCHÆOLOGICAL SKETCHES IN SCOTLAND.

BY CAPT. T. P. WHITE, R.E., &c.

VOL. II., KNAPDALE, GIGHA, &c.  With 130 Illustrations.  Folio.

# THEOLOGICAL WORKS.

**Caird—SERMONS.**
By JOHN CAIRD, D.D., Principal of the University of Glasgow. Thirteenth Thousand. Fcap. 8vo, 5s.

"They are noble sermons; and we are not sure but that, with the cultivated reader, they will gain rather than lose by being read, not heard. There is a thoughtfulness and depth about them which can hardly be appreciated, unless when they are studied at leisure; and there are so many sentences so felicitously expressed that we should grudge being hurried away from them by a rapid speaker, without being allowed to enjoy them a second time."—*Fraser's Magazine.*

—— **RELIGION IN COMMON LIFE:**
A Sermon preached in Crathie Church, October 14, 1855, before Her Majesty the Queen and Prince Albert. By the SAME. Published by Her Majesty's Command. Bound in cloth, 8d. Cheap Edition, 3d.

**Campbell—THE THEORY OF RULING ELDERSHIP;**
Or, The Position of the Lay Ruler in the Reformed Churches Examined. By P. C. CAMPBELL, D.D., Principal of the University of Aberdeen. 3s.

"Principal Campbell deserves the best thanks of the whole community for setting forth the subject so opportunely, and in a work so lucid in arrangement, so accurate in statement, so irresistible in reasoning, and so perspicuous and pleasing in style. We most heartily recommend his production to the most anxious attention of the Churches and the public generally."—*Glasgow Herald.*

**Charteris —NOTES ON SOME PRESENT-DAY ATTACKS**
ON THE CHRISTIAN DOCTRINE. A Lecture Delivered at the Opening of the Theological class in Edinburgh University, Session 1870-71. By the REV. PROFESSOR CHARTERIS. 8vo, 1s.

**Church of Scotland—THE ANNUAL VOLUME OF REPORTS**
OF THE SCHEMES OF THE CHURCH. Price 1s. 6d., bound in cloth.

—— THE CHURCH OF SCOTLAND HOME AND
FOREIGN MISSIONARY RECORD; Containing Reports of the Missions of the Church, Lists of Contributions on Account of the Schemes, and Ecclesiastical Intelligence. Published on the First Day of each Month. Three halfpence.

—— FAMILY PRAYERS.
Authorised by the General Assembly of the Church of Scotland. A New Edition, crown, 8vo, in large type. 4s. 6d.
ANOTHER EDITION, crown 8vo, 2s.

**Church of Scotland**—PRAYERS FOR SOCIAL AND FAMILY
WORSHIP. For the Use of Soldiers, Sailors, Colonists, and Sojourners
in India, and other persons, at home and abroad, who are deprived of the
ordinary services of a Christian Ministry. Cheap Edition, 1s. 6d.

—— THE SCOTTISH HYMNAL.
HYMNS FOR PUBLIC WORSHIP, Published for Use in Churches by Authority of the General Assembly.

1. Large type, cloth, red edges, 1s. 6d. ; French morocco, 2s. 6d. ; calf, 6s.
2. Bourgeois type, cloth, red edges, 1s. ; French morocco, 2s.
3. Minion type, limp. cloth, 6d. ; French morocco, 1s. 6d.
4. School Edition, in paper cover, 2d.
     No. 1, bound with the Psalms and Paraphrases, cloth, 3s. ; French
     morocco, 4s. 6d. ; calf, 7s. 6d.
     No. 2, bound with the Psalms and Paraphrases, cloth, 2s. ; French
     morocco, 3s.

—— THE SCOTTISH HYMNAL, WITH MUSIC.
Selected by the Committees on Hymns and on Psalmody. The harmonies
arranged by W. H. Monk, cloth, 1s. 6d. ; French morocco, 3s. 6d. The
same in the Tonic Sol-fa Notation, 1s. 6d. and 3s. 6d.
An Edition with fixed Tune for each Hymn, cloth, 3s. 6d. French
morocco, 5s. 6d.

—— INDEX TO THE ACTS OF THE GENERAL ASSEMBLY
OF THE CHURCH OF SCOTLAND. From the Revolution to the
present time. By the REV. JOHN WILSON, Dunning. A New Edition,
brought down to 1870. Crown 8vo, 5s.

**Cochrane**—THE RESURRECTION OF THE DEAD:
Its Design, Manner, and Results. In an Exposition of the Fifteenth Chapter
of First Corinthians. By the REV. JAMES COCHRANE, D.D., Minister
of the First Parochial Charge, Cupar-Fife ; Author of ' The World to Come,'
' Discourses on Difficult Texts of Scripture,' &c. In crown 8vo, 7s. 6d.

"Rarely have we come across a more discriminating exposition of that marvellous chapter, the
15th of 1st Corinthians, than that by Mr Cochrane."—*John Bull.*
"It is a work of much ability, lucid, argumentative, often rising to eloquence, and full of
interest."—*Armagh Guardian.*
"The characteristic of the volume is strong, clear-headed, sober good sense."—*British Quarterly
Review.*

**Cotterill**—THE GENESIS OF THE CHURCH.
By the RIGHT REV. HENRY COTTERILL, D.D., Bishop of Edinburgh.
Demy 8vo, 16s.

"The book is strikingly original, and this originality is one of its great charms—the views of an
able and cultivated man whom long study has made fully master of his subject."—*Scottish Guardian.*
"In Dr Cotterill's volume a book of great ability has been presented to the world."—*Edinburgh
Courant.*
"This book breathes the spirit and is stamped with the character of the present age. It requires,
and will amply repay, the most careful and attentive reading ; and it is likely to carry conviction to
many a mind which has been merely repelled by the ordinary quoting of texts or appeals to Church
History to prove the existence of the three Orders, and the necessity of the apostolical succession."—*Literary Churchman.*
"It is a very able book, and has the high merit in our eyes of appealing directly to New Testament authority ; its separate expositions and arguments are acute in perception, moderate in
position, and candid in spirit."—*British Quarterly Review.*

**Crawford**—THE FATHERHOOD OF GOD:
Considered in its General and Special Aspects, and particularly in relation
to the Atonement; with a Review of Recent Speculations on the Subject.
By THOMAS J. CRAWFORD, D.D., Professor of Divinity in the
University of Edinburgh. Third Edition, revised and enlarged, with a
Reply to the Strictures of Dr Candlish. 9s.

"The plan of this work is comprehensive and yet definite. It embodies much original thought,
and the author's habits of searching inquiry and careful arrangement stand him in good stead.
Whatever difference of opinion there may be on sundry topics, it would be idle to question the
great ability shown by the learned Professor. As the subjects treated of have been and are so
much discussed, it will be satisfactory to many to receive a book which expounds so fully, and
maintains so forcibly, and on a Scriptural basis, the views of one so well qualified to speak."—
*Journal of Sacred Literature.*

———— THE DOCTRINE OF HOLY SCRIPTURE RESPECT-
ING THE ATONEMENT. By the SAME. 8vo, 12s.

"This addition to the latest contributions to the elucidation of the doctrine of the atonement
must inevitably take a high rank among them. It collates and analyzes the teachings, not only of
the apostles, but of all Scriptural authors on the subject. The work is done in a critical, thorough,
exhaustive manner, and gives us an exhaustive thesaurus of Scriptural doctrine on the subject."—
*Princeton Review.*

———— PRESBYTERIANISM DEFENDED AGAINST THE
EXCLUSIVE CLAIMS OF PRELACY, as urged by Romanists and
Tractarians. By the SAME. Second Edition. Also, PRESBYTERY OR
PRELACY, which is the more conformable to the pattern of the Apostolic
Churches? By the SAME. Second Edition. Bound in one volume, 2s.

**Cumming**—FROM PATMOS TO PARADISE;
Or, Light on the Past, the Present, and the Future. By the REV. JOHN
CUMMING, D.D., F.R.S.E., Minister of the Scotch National Church,
Crown Court, Covent Garden, London. Crown 8vo, 7s. 6d.

**Davidson**—BELIEF—WHAT IS IT?
Or, The Nature of Faith as Determined by the Facts of Human Nature and
Sacred History. By REV. JOHN DAVIDSON, M.A. 8vo, 7s.

THE DIVINE FOOTSTEPS IN HUMAN HISTORY.
8vo, 10s. 6d.

THE DOCTRINE OF THE CHURCH OF SCOTLAND ON
THE SACRAMENTS, Extracted from her Standards, as a Text-Book for
the Instruction of Young Persons preparing for their first Communion. 2d.
Twelve copies for 1s. 6d.

**Edgar**—SCHEME OF LESSONS FOR SUNDAY SCHOOLS
AND BIBLE CLASSES FOR THE FIRST, SECOND, AND THIRD YEARS.
By the REV. ROBERT EDGAR, M.A., Newburgh. 3s. per Hundred.

———— NOTES, CRITICAL AND EXPLANATORY, TO AID TEACHERS
IN USING THE ABOVE SCHEME OF LESSONS. By the SAME. 8vo,
in three parts, one for each Year's Lessons. 4s. 6d.

EUCHOLOGION ; or, A Book of Common Order.
Being Forms of Worship issued by The Church Service Society. A
New and Revised Edition, being the Third.      [*In the Press.*

Flint—CHRIST'S KINGDOM UPON EARTH.
By the Rev. ROBERT FLINT, Professor of Moral Philosophy in the
University of St Andrews. Crown 8vo, 7s. 6d.

Hay—THE WORKS OF THE RIGHT REV. BISHOP HAY,
of Edinburgh. Together with a Memoir of the Author, and Portrait
engraved from the Painting at the College of Blairs. Edited under the
supervision of the Right Rev. Bishop STRAIN. A New Edition, in
5 vols. Crown 8vo, 21s.

"The works derive interest from the character and career of the writer, but they have an in-
dependent value as one of the finest expositions in English of the doctrines of the Catholic
Church."—*Cork Examiner.*
"We have before us, in five volumes, published in the most finished style of typography, the
invaluable works of Bishop Hay, of Edinburgh, which form the most complete and clear enuncia-
tion of Catholic doctrine, practice, and piety ever written in the language."—*Liverpool Catholic
Times.*
"In fact, we should say of these five volumes that they form an invaluable collection for both
priest and layman ; and we augur for them, on account of their intrinsic worth and of the immense
benefits they have already conferred, a widespread sale."—*Tablet.*

—— BISHOP HAY ON MIRACLES.
The Scripture Doctrine of Miracles Displayed, in which they are impartially
examined and explained, according to the Light of Revelation and the
Principles of Sound Reason. By the Right Rev. Dr GEORGE HAY,
Bishop of Edinburgh. 2 vols. crown 8vo, 10s. 6d.

"The work is the product of great learning scriptural and scholastic, and it is a model in its
method. . . . . It is of the profoundest interest, whether to those who accept the belief they
are intended to enforce, or to those who may honestly dissent from it."—*Cork Examiner.*
"The survey of the subject is remarkably comprehensive, and the handling of it very able.
The volumes are well worth reading."—*Literary Churchman.*

Hill—LECTURES IN DIVINITY.
By Rev. GEORGE HILL, D.D., Principal of St Mary's College, St
Andrews. Stereotyped Edition. 8vo, 14s.
"I am not sure if I can recommend a more complete manual of Divinity."—*Dr Chalmers.*

Hill—THE PRACTICE IN THE SEVERAL JUDICATORIES
OF THE CHURCH OF SCOTLAND. By ALEXANDER HILL,
D.D. Sixth Edition, fcap. 8vo, 4s.

Hutchison—SERMONS.
By GEORGE HUTCHISON, D.D., Minister of Banchory-Ternan. 8vo,
8s. 6d.

Jamieson—THE INSPIRATION OF THE HOLY SCRIP-
TURES. Being the Baird Lectures for 1873. By the Rev. ROBERT
JAMIESON, D.D. In one volume, crown 8vo, 7s. 6d.

**Joceline**—THE MOTHER'S LEGACIE TO HER UNBORNE CHILDE. By Mrs ELIZABETH JOCELINE. Edited by the Very Rev. Principal LEE. Cloth, gilt edges, 32mo, 4s. 6d. Also in morocco antique, 8s. 6d.

"This beautiful and touching Legacie."—*Athenæum.*
"A delightful monument of the piety and high feeling of a truly noble mother."—*Morning Advertiser.*

**Knox**—JOHN KNOX'S LITURGY:
THE BOOK OF COMMON ORDER, AND THE DIRECTORY FOR PUBLIC WORSHIP OF THE CHURCH OF SCOTLAND. With Historical Introductions and Illustrative Notes by the Rev. GEORGE W. SPROTT, B.A., and the Rev. THOMAS LEISHMAN. D.D. Handsomely printed, in imitation of the large editions of Andro Hart, on toned paper, bound in cloth, red edges, 8s. 6d.

"We heartily recommend Mr Sprott's Introduction to the 'Book of Common Order' to every one who wishes honestly to get the truth, and the whole truth, about the history, so far as Scotland is concerned, concerning a devotional formulary which has had so curious a destiny. This Introduction is full of learning, used with a candour that deserves all honour. In reading it we cannot find whether the author is a supporter or an opponent of a formulary of worship—he has undertaken the history of one book of that kind, and he tells it fairly out."—*Scotsman.*

**Lee**—LECTURES ON THE HISTORY OF THE CHURCH OF SCOTLAND, FROM THE REFORMATION TO THE REVOLUTION SETTLEMENT. By the late Very Rev. JOHN LEE, D.D., LL.D., Principal of the University of Edinburgh. With Notes and Appendices from the Author's Papers. Edited by the Rev. WILLIAM LEE, D.D. Two vols. 8vo, 21s.

—— PASTORAL ADDRESSES OF THE GENERAL ASSEMBLY OF THE CHURCH OF SCOTLAND. By the Same. Fcap. 8vo, 2s. 6d.

—— INAUGURAL ADDRESSES IN THE UNIVERSITY OF EDINBURGH. By the Same. To which is prefixed a Memoir by Lord Neaves. Fcap. 8vo, 2s. 6d.

**Lee**—THE INCREASE OF FAITH. By WILLIAM LEE, D.D. Second Edition, 4s.

"A large work in a very small compass. . . . The subject is most important. It touches many questions of practical controversy, and questions, moreover, with which a practical ministry has constantly to deal . . . It is scarcely possible to speak too highly of the way in which the task has been executed."—*Rev. E. Garbett's Christian Advocate.*

—— THE DAYS OF THE SON OF MAN: A History of the Church in the Time of Our Lord. By the Same. Crown 8vo, 6s. 6d.

"We welcome this volume, and most cordially recommend it to all intelligent and earnest students of the word of God."—*United Presbyterian Magazine.*
"Dr Lee's thoughtful little book deserves high commendation. . . . As a manual for family and school use it is, we think, the very best that has come under our notice."—*British Quarterly Review.*

—— THE DUTIES OF ELDERS IN THE CHURCH OF SCOTLAND. With an Examination of Prevalent Objections to an Acceptance of the Office. By the Same. 4d.

**M'Culloch—SERMONS.**
By JAMES M'CULLOCH, D.D., Minister of West Kirk, Greenock. Second Edition. 8vo, 6s.

"While the graces of the author's composition will be admired by those who appreciate the beauties of diction, the evangelical and decidedly practical character of the discourses must make them exceedingly acceptable to all Christian readers."—*North British Daily Mail.*
"We have seen no volume of Sermons of recent publication which has greater claims upon attention, or is more worthy of perusal."—*Courant.*

**Maclachlan—NOTES ON THE PARABLES,**
According to Literal and Futurist Principles of Interpretation. By MAS MACLACHLAN (of Maclachlan). Crown 8vo, 4s.

*By the Same Author.*

NOTES ON THE UNFULFILLED PROPHECIES OF ISAIAH. Post 8vo, 8s. 6d.

NOTES ON THE BOOK OF REVELATION. Post 8vo, 6s.

NOTES ON REFERENCES AND QUOTATIONS IN THE NEW TESTAMENT SCRIPTURES FROM THE OLD TESTAMENT. Post 8vo, 8s. 6d.

**M'Letchie—SERMONS AND DISCOURSES.**
By the late REV. JAMES M'LETCHIE, D.D., High Church, Edinburgh. With Portrait, and a Memoir by the Rev. Dr MACRAE. 10s. 6d.

**Macpherson—THE RESURRECTION OF JESUS CHRIST:**
With an Examination of the Speculations of Strauss in his 'New Life of Jesus,' and an Introductory View of the Present Position of Theological Inquiry in reference to the Existence of God, and the Miraculous Evidence of Christianity. By the late ROBERT MACPHERSON, D.D., Professor of Theology in the University of Aberdeen. 8vo, 9s.

"The patience and candour of the author in following Strauss into all the sophistical sinuosities of his unbelief are remarkable, and the signal ability with which his theories are refuted makes his book valuable as an armoury of true weapons against much of the infidelity of the day."—*Christian Witness.*

**Murray—THE PROPHET'S MANTLE:**
Being Scenes from the Life of Elisha, Son of Shaphat. By the REV. JAMES MURRAY, Minister of Old Cumnock. Crown 8vo, 4s. 6d.

"These discourses may be recommended as models of brevity, elegant writing, and sound teaching."—*Christian Times.*
"Singularly attractive."—*The Spectator.*

**Nicholson—REST IN JESUS.**
By the REV. MAXWELL NICHOLSON, D.D., Edinburgh. Fourth Edition. Fcap. 8vo, 4s. 6d.

"Any one in search of a book for quiet reading, and on evangelical principles, will not be disappointed in the one now before us. . . . Very beautifully written. . . . Altogether practical and experimental."—*Journal of Sacred Literature.*
"Bright, truthful, and consolatory."—*Eclectic Review.*

**Paul—ANALYSIS AND CRITICAL INTERPRETATION OF THE HEBREW TEXT OF THE BOOK OF GENESIS.** Preceded by a Hebrew Grammar, and Dissertations on the Genuineness of the Pentateuch, and on the Structure of the Hebrew Language. By the REV. WILLIAM PAUL, A.M. 8vo, 18s.

**THE PHILOSOPHY OF CHRISTIANITY: OR THE PURPOSE AND POWER OF THE GOSPEL.** Crown 8vo, 5s.

**Pirie**—NATURAL THEOLOGY;

An Inquiry into the Fundamental Principles of Religious, Moral, and Political Science. By W. R. PIRIE, D.D., Professor of Divinity and Church History in the University of Aberdeen. 5s.

**Robertson**—LIFE OF THE LATE REV. JAMES ROBERTSON, D.D., F.R.S.E., Professor of Divinity and Ecclesiastical History in the University of Edinburgh. By PROFESSOR CHARTERIS. With Portrait. 8vo, 10s. 6d.

"This is a beautiful record of the life of a true man. . . . Mr Charteris has discharged the duty of biographer with fidelity and candour, with rare good taste, and an affectionate reverence. The memoir is worthy of its subject, and supplies one of the most interesting biographies which has seen the light for many a day."—*Aberdeen Free Press.*

**Sellar**—CHURCH DOCTRINE AND PRACTICE.

A Series of Sermons. By the Rev. JAMES A. SELLAR, A.M., Incumbent of St Peter's (Episcopal) Church, Edinburgh. Crown 8vo, 6s. 6d.

**Tholuck**—HOURS OF CHRISTIAN DEVOTION.

Translated from the German of A. THOLUCK, D.D., Professor of Theology in the University of Halle, and Councillor of the Supreme Consistory, Prussia. By the REV. ROBERT MENZIES, D.D. With a Preface written for this Translation by the Author. Crown 8vo, 9s.

"To many of these meditations four or five great texts are prefixed, and the reader feels that the gentle pressure of a powerful hand has crushed these sacred fruits, and handed him the fragrant wine of the kingdom in a golden goblet. . . . The abundance and variety of the material furnished in this volume for quiet pondering render further characterisation difficult. We are thankful for the introduction of this wise, thoughtful, helpful book in this dark, sad season."—*British Quarterly Review.*

**Tulloch**—RATIONAL THEOLOGY AND CHRISTIAN PHILOSOPHY IN ENGLAND IN THE SEVENTEENTH CENTURY. By JOHN TULLOCH, D.D. Second Edition. 2 vols. 8vo, 28s.

"The pleasure with which Principal Tulloch explores this comparatively unknown field recommends itself to his readers, and the academic groves of Oxford and Cambridge are invested with the freshness of a new glory."—*Edinburgh Review.*

"It is rich in pregnant and suggestive thought."—*Athenæum.*

"Ample scholarship, well-disciplined powers, catholic sympathies, and a masculine eloquence, give it a high place among modern contributions to theological science."—*British Quarterly Review.*

"From his lively portraits they will learn to know some of the finest spirits England has produced; while from his able and comprehensive summaries of the works they left behind them, any reader of quick intelligence may acquaint himself with their leading thoughts."—*Nonconformist.*

—— LEADERS OF THE REFORMATION:

Luther, Calvin, Latimer, and Knox. By the SAME. Second Edition, crown 8vo. New Edition in preparation.

—— ENGLISH PURITANISM AND ITS LEADERS;

CROMWELL, MILTON, BAXTER, and BUNYAN. By the SAME. Uniform with the 'Leaders of the Reformation.' New Edition in preparation.

——THEISM.

The Witness of Reason and Nature to an All-Wise and Beneficent Creator. By the SAME. 8vo, 10s. 6d.

"Dr Tulloch's Essay, in its masterly statement of the real nature and difficulties of the subject, its logical exactness in distinguishing the illustrative from the suggestive, its lucid arrangement of the argument, its simplicity of expression, is quite unequalled by any work we have seen on the subject."—*Christian Remembrancer.*

# EDUCATIONAL WORKS.

## ANCIENT CLASSICS FOR ENGLISH READERS.
### Edited by the REV. W. LUCAS COLLINS, M.A.

The Volumes already published are :—

HOMER'S ILIAD. By Rev. W. L. Collins, M.A.
HOMER'S ODYSSEY. By the Same.
HERODOTUS. By G. C. Swayne, M.A.
CÆSAR. By Anthony Trollope.
VIRGIL. By Rev. W. L. Collins, M.A.
HORACE. By Theodore Martin.
ÆSCHYLUS. By R. S. Copleston, B.A.
XENOPHON. By Sir Alex. Grant, Bart.
CICERO. By Rev. W. L. Collins, M.A.
SOPHOCLES. By C. W. Collins, M.A.

PLINY. By Rev. A. Church, M.A., and Rev. W. J. Brodribb, M.A.
EURIPIDES. By W. B. Donne, M.A.
JUVENAL. By E. Walford, M.A.
ARISTOPHANES. By the Editor.
HESIOD. By Rev. James Davies, M.A.
PLAUTUS AND TERENCE. By the Editor.
TACITUS. By W. B. Donne, M.A.
LUCIAN. By the Editor.
PLATO. By Clifton W. Collins.

A Volume of this Series is published Quarterly, 2s. 6d.

"It is difficult to estimate too highly the value of such a series as this in giving 'English readers' an insight, exact as far as it goes, into those olden times which are so remote and yet to many of us so close. It is in no wise to be looked upon as a rival to the translations which have at no time been brought forth in greater abundance or in greater excellence than in our own day. On the contrary, we should hope that these little volumes would be in many cases but a kind of stepping-stone to the larger works, and would lead many who otherwise would have remained in ignorance of them to turn to the versions of Conington, Worsley, Derby, or Lytton. In any case a reader would come with far greater knowledge, and therefore with far greater enjoyment, to the complete translation, who had first had the ground broken for him by one of these volumes."—*Saturday Review.*

## Brown—ADVANCED TEXT-BOOK OF BOTANY.
For the Use of Students. By ROBERT BROWN, M.A., PH.D., F.R.G.S., Lecturer on Botany under the Science and Art Department of Committee of the Privy Council on Education. [*In the Press.*

## Cauvin—A TREASURY OF THE ENGLISH AND GERMAN
LANGUAGES. Compiled from the best Authors and Lexicographers in both Languages. Adapted to the Use of Schools, Students, Travellers, and Men of Business ; and forming a Companion to all German-English Dictionaries. By JOSEPH CAUVIN, LL.D. & PH.D., of the University of Göttingen, &c. Crown 8vo, 7s. 6d.; bound in cloth.

"An excellent English-German Dictionary, which supplies a real want."—*Saturday Review.*
"The difficulty of translating English into German may be greatly alleviated by the use of this copious and excellent English-German Dictionary, which specifies the different senses of each English word, and gives suitable German equivalents. It also supplies an abundance of idiomatic phraseology, with many passages from Shakespeare and other authors aptly rendered in German. Compared with other dictionaries, it has decidedly the advantage."—*Athenæum.*

**Currie**—ENGLISH PROSE COMPOSITION :
A Practical Manual for Use in Schools. By JAMES CURRIE, M.A.,
Principal of the Church of Scotland Training College, Edinburgh. Ninth
Edition, 1s. 6d.

"We do not remember having seen a work so completely to our mind as this, which combines
sound theory with judicious practice. Proceeding step by step, it advances from the formation
of the shortest sentences to the composition of complete essays, the pupil being everywhere
furnished with all needful assistance in the way of models and hints. Nobody can work through
such a book as this without thoroughly understanding the structure of sentences, and acquiring
facility in arranging and expressing his thoughts appropriately. It ought to be extensively used."
—*Athenæum.*

**Harbord**—A GLOSSARY OF NAVIGATION.
Containing the Definitions and Propositions of the Science, Explanation of
Terms, and Description of Instrument. By the REV. J. B. HARBORD,
M.A., Assistant Director of Education, Admiralty. Crown 8vo, Illustrated
with Diagrams, 6s.

—— DEFINITIONS AND DIAGRAMS IN ASTRONOMY
AND NAVIGATION. By the SAME. 1s. 6d.

**Lockwood**—PROGRESSIVE AND CLASSIFIED SPELLING-
BOOK. By HANNAH R. LOCKWOOD, Authoress of 'Little Mary's
Mythology.' Fcap. 8vo, 1s.

**Mackay**—A MANUAL OF MODERN GEOGRAPHY.
Mathematical, Physical, and Political. By the REV. ALEXANDER
MACKAY, LL.D., F.R.G.S. New and greatly Improved Edition. Crown
8vo, pp. 676, 7s. 6d.
This volume—the result of many years' unremitting application—is specially
adapted for the use of Teachers, Advanced Classes, Candidates for the Civil
Service, and proficients in geography generally.

"Of all the manuals on Geography that have come under our notice, we place the one whose
title is given above in the first rank. For fulness of information, for knowledge of method in
arrangement, for the manner in which the details are handled, we know of no work that can, in
these respects, compete with Dr Mackay's Manual."—*English Journal of Education.*

—— ELEMENTS OF MODERN GEOGRAPHY.
By the SAME. Thirteenth Edition, revised to the present time. Crown
8vo, pp. 300. 3s.
The 'Elements' form a careful condensation of the 'Manual,' the order of
arrangement being the same, the river-systems of the globe playing the same
conspicuous part, the pronunciation being given, and the results of the latest census
being uniformly exhibited. This volume is now extensively introduced into many
of the best schools in the kingdom.

"The best Geography we have ever met with."—*Spectator.*

—— OUTLINES OF MODERN GEOGRAPHY.
Fifteenth Edition, revised to the present time. By the SAME. 18mo, pp.
112. 1s.
These 'Outlines'—in many respects an epitome of the 'Elements'—are carefully
prepared to meet the wants of beginners. The arrangement is the same as in the
Author's larger works. Minute details are avoided, the broad outlines are graphi-
cally presented, the accentuation marked, and the most recent changes in political
geography exhibited.

**Mackay**—FIRST STEPS IN GEOGRAPHY.
> Forty-first thousand, revised to the present time. By the SAME. 18mo, pp. 56. Sewed, 4d. In cloth, 6d.

―――― GEOGRAPHY OF THE BRITISH EMPIRE.
> From 'First Steps in Geography.' By the SAME. 3d.

―――― FACTS AND DATES;
> or, The Leading Events in Sacred and Profane History, and the Principal Facts in the Various Physical Sciences; the Memory being aided through-out by a Simple and Natural Method. For Schools and Private Reference. By the SAME. Second Edition, crown 8vo, pp. 336. 4s.

**Michie**—THE LIFE AND LABOURS OF THE APOSTLE
> PAUL. A continuous Narrative for School and Bible Classes. By CHARLES MICHIE, M.A., Author of an 'Outline of the Geography of Palestine.' 1s., with a Map.

**Minto**—A MANUAL OF ENGLISH PROSE LITERATURE,
> Biographical and Critical; designed mainly to show Characteristics of Style. By W. MINTO, M.A. Crown 8vo, 10s. 6d.

> "It is a work which all who desire to make a close study of style in English prose will do well to use attentively."—*Standard.*
> "Here we do not find the crude reptile of old critical formulæ, the simple echoes of super-annuated rhetorical dicta, but a clear and careful analysis of the main attributes of style, as developed in the work of its greatest masters, stated with remarkable clearness of expression, and arranged upon a plan of most exact method. Nothing can be well conceived more consummate as a matter of skill than the analytical processes of the writer as he lays bare to our view the whole anatomy—even every joint and sinew and artery in the frameworks—of the sentence he dissects, and as he points out their reciprocal relations, their minute interdependencies."—*School Board Chronicle.*
> "An admirable book, well selected and well put together."—*Westminster Review.*

―――― CHARACTERISTICS OF ENGLISH POETS,
> From Chaucer to Shirley. By the SAME. 1 vol. crown 8vo. [*In the Press.*

**Munn**—THE THEORY OF ARITHMETIC.
> By DAVID MUNN, F.R.S.E., Mathematical Master, Royal High School of Edinburgh. Crown 8vo, pp. 294. 5s.

> "We want books of this kind very much—books which aim at developing the educational value of Arithmetic by showing how admirably it is calculated to exercise the thinking powers of the young. Your book is, I think, excellent—brief but clear; and I look forward to the good effects which it shall produce, in weaking the minds of many who regard Arithmetic as a mere mechanical process."—*Professor Kelland.*

**Nicholson**—A MANUAL OF ZOOLOGY,
> For the use of Students. With a General Introduction on the Principles of Zoology. By HENRY ALLEYNE NICHOLSON, M.D., F.R.S.E., F.G.S., &c., Professor of Zoology in the Royal College of Science, Dublin. Third Edition. Crown 8vo, pp. 706, with 250 Engravings on Wood, 12s. 6d.

> "It is the best manual of Zoology yet published, not merely in England, but in Europe."—*Pall Mall Gazette.*
> "The best treatise on Zoology in moderate compass that we possess."—*Lancet.*

**Nicholson—ADVANCED TEXT-BOOK OF ZOOLOGY.**
By the SAME. Second Edition, Enlarged. Crown 8vo, 6s.

"The author's text-book is a decided success; it is just what was wanted. The subject has been treated in a scientific spirit, but at the same time so clearly and well as to be quite within the comprehension of any young student who will bring ordinary attention to his task."—*Lancet.*

—— INTRODUCTORY TEXT-BOOK OF ZOOLOGY FOR
SCHOOLS. A New Edition. By the SAME. Crown 8vo, 2s. 6d.

"Nothing can be better adapted to its object than this cheap and well written introduction."—*London Quarterly Review.*

—— OUTLINES OF NATURAL HISTORY,
For Beginners; being Descriptions of a Progressive Series of Zoological Types. By the SAME. 52 Engravings, 1s. 6d.

"There has been no book since Patterson's well-known 'Zoology for Schools' that has so completely provided for the class to which it is addressed as the capital little volume by Dr Nicholson."—*Popular Science Review.*

—— EXAMINATIONS IN NATURAL HISTORY;
Being a Progressive Series of Questions adapted to the Author's Introductory and Advanced Text-Books and the Student's Manual of Zoology. By the SAME. 1s.

—— INTRODUCTION TO THE STUDY OF BIOLOGY.
By the SAME. Crown 8vo, with numerous Engravings, 5s.

"Admirably written and fairly illustrated, and brings within the compass of 160 pages the record of investigations and discoveries scattered over so many volumes. Seldom indeed do we find such subjects treated in a style at once so popular and yet so minutely accurate in scientific detail."—*Scotsman.*

—— A MANUAL OF PALÆONTOLOGY,
For the Use of Students. By the SAME. Crown 8vo, with upwards of 400 Engravings, 15s.

"One of the best of guides to the principles of Palæontology and the study of organic remains."—*Athenæum.*

**Page—INTRODUCTORY TEXT-BOOK OF GEOLOGY.**
By DAVID PAGE, LL.D., Professor of Geology in the Durham University of Physical Science, Newcastle. With Engravings on Wood and Glossarial Index. Tenth Edition, Enlarged, 2s. 6d.

"It has not been our good fortune to examine a text-book on science of which we could express an opinion so entirely favourable as we are enabled to do of Dr Page's little work."—*Athenæum.*

—— ADVANCED TEXT-BOOK OF GEOLOGY,
Descriptive and Industrial. By the SAME. With Engravings and Glossary of Scientific Terms. Fifth Edition, Revised and Enlarged, 7s. 6d.

"We have carefully read this truly satisfactory book, and do not hesitate to say that it is an excellent compendium of the great facts of Geology, and written in a truthful and philosophic spirit."—*Edinburgh Philosophical Journal.*
"As a school-book nothing can match the 'Advanced Text-Book of Geology' by Professor Page of Newcastle."—*Mechanic's Magazine.*

—— THE GEOLOGICAL EXAMINATOR.
A Progressive Series of Questions, adapted to the Introductory and Advanced Text-Books of Geology. Prepared to assist Teachers in framing their Examinations, and Students in testing their own Progress and Proficiency. By the SAME. Fifth Edition. 9d.

**Page** — SYNOPSES OF SUBJECTS TAUGHT IN THE GEOLOGICAL CLASS, College of Physical Science, Newcastle-on-Tyne, University of Durham. By the SAME. Fcap., cloth, 2s. 6d.

——— HANDBOOK OF GEOLOGICAL TERMS, GEOLOGY, AND PHYSICAL GEOGRAPHY. By the SAME. Second Edition, Enlarged, 7s. 6d.

——— THE PHILOSOPHY OF GEOLOGY. A Brief Review of the Aim, Scope, and Character of Geological Inquiry. By the SAME. Fcap. 8vo, 3s. 6d.

"The great value of Mr Page's volume is its suggestive character. The problems he discusses are the highest and most interesting in the science—those on which it most becomes the thinkers and the leaders of the age to make up their minds. The time is now past for geologists to observe silence on these matters, and in this way to depreciate at once the interest and importance of their investigations. It is well to know that, however they may decide, questions of high philosophy are at stake, and therefore we give a hearty welcome to every book which, like Mr Page's, discusses these questions in a fair and liberal spirit."—*Scotsman.*

——— GEOLOGY FOR GENERAL READERS. A Series of Popular Sketches in Geology and Palæontology. By the SAME. Third Edition, enlarged, 6s.

"This is one of the best of Dr Page's many good books. It is written in a flowing popular style. Without illustration or any extraneous aid, the narrative must prove attractive to any intelligent reader."—*Geological Magazine.*

——— CHIPS AND CHAPTERS. A Book for Amateurs and Young Geologists. By the SAME. 5s.

——— THE PAST AND PRESENT LIFE OF THE GLOBE. With numerous Illustrations. By the SAME. Crown 8vo, 6s.

——— THE CRUST OF THE EARTH : A Handy Outline of Geology. By the SAME. Sixth Edition. 1s.

"An eminently satisfactory work, giving, in less than 100 pages, an admirable outline sketch of Geology, . . . forming, if not a royal road, at least one of the smoothest we possess to an intelligent acquaintance with geological phenomena."—*Scotsman.*

——— ECONOMIC GEOLOGY ; OR, GEOLOGY IN ITS RELATIONS TO THE ARTS AND MANUFACTURES. By the SAME.                    [*In the Press.*

——— INTRODUCTORY TEXT-BOOK OF PHYSICAL GEOGRAPHY. With Sketch-Maps and Illustrations. By the SAME. Fifth Edition, Enlarged, 2s. 6d.

"Whether as a school-book or a manual for the private student, this work has no equal in our Educational literature."—*Iron.*

——— ADVANCED TEXT-BOOK OF PHYSICAL GEO-GRAPHY. By the SAME. With Engravings. Second Edition, Enlarged, 5s.

"A thoroughly good Text-Book of Physical Geography."—*Saturday Review.*

**Page**— EXAMINATIONS ON PHYSICAL GEOGRAPHY.
A Progressive Series of Questions, adapted to the Introductory and Advanced Text-Books of Physical Geography. By DAVID PAGE, LL.D., &c. Second Edition. 9d.

**Ritter**—COMPARATIVE GEOGRAPHY.
By CARL RITTER. Translated by W. L. GAGE. Fcap., 3s. 6d.

**Rossiter**—ELEMENTARY HANDBOOK OF PHYSICS.
With 210 Diagrams. By WILLIAM ROSSITER, F.R.A.S., &c. Crown 8vo, pp. 390. 5s.

"A singularly interesting Treatise on Physics, founded on facts and phenomena gained at first hand by the author, and expounded in a style which is a model of that simplicity and ease in writing which betokens mastery of the subject. To those who require a non-mathematical exposition of the principles of Physics, a better book cannot be recommended."—*Pall Mall Gazette.*

**Sang**—ELEMENTARY ARITHMETIC.
By EDWARD SANG, F.R.S.E. This Treatise is intended to apply the great desideratum of an intellectual instead of a routine course of instruction in Arithmetic. Post 8vo, 5s.

———— THE HIGHER ARITHMETIC.
By the SAME. Being a Sequel to 'Elementary Arithmetic.' Crown 8vo, 5s.

**Stewart**—A CONCISE HEBREW GRAMMAR;
With the Pronunciation, Syllabic Division and Tone of the Words, and Quantity of the Vowels. By the REV. DUNCAN STEWART, B.A. 8vo, cloth, limp, 3s.

**Stormonth**—ETYMOLOGICAL AND PRONOUNCING DICTIONARY OF THE ENGLISH LANGUAGE. Including a very Copious Selection of Scientific Terms. For Use in Schools and Colleges, and as a Book of General Reference. By the REV. JAMES STORMONTH. The Pronunciation carefully Revised by the Rev. P. H. PHELP, M.A., Cantab. Crown 8vo, pp. 775, 7s. 6d.

"This dictionary is admirable. It deserves a place in every English School."—*Westminster Review.*

———— THE SCHOOL ETYMOLOGICAL DICTIONARY AND WORD-BOOK. Combining the advantages of an ordinary Pronouncing School Dictionary and an Etymological Spelling-Book. By the SAME. Fcap. 8vo, pp. 254, 2s.

"The derivations are particularly good."—*Westminster Review.*

**Sandford**—THE GREEK GRAMMAR OF THIERSCH.
Translated from the German, with Brief Remarks. By SIR DANIEL K. SANDFORD, M.A., Professor of Greek in the University of Glasgow. 8vo, 16s.

**White**—THE EIGHTEEN CHRISTIAN CENTURIES.
By the REV. JAMES WHITE. Seventh Edition, post 8vo, with Index, 6s.

———— HISTORY OF FRANCE,
FROM THE EARLIEST TIMES. By the SAME. Fifth Edition, post 8vo, with Index, 6s.

# AGRICULTURE, GARDENING, &c.

— ◆ —

**Ainslie**—AINSLIE'S TREATISE ON LAND SURVEYING.
A New and Enlarged Edition, edited by WILLIAM GALBRAITH, M.A.,
F.R.A.S. 1 vol. 8vo, with a volume of Plates in 4to, 21s.

**Brown**—THE FORESTER :
A Practical Treatise on the Planting, Rearing, and General Management of
Forest-trees. By JAMES BROWN, Wood-Surveyor and Nurseryman,
Stirling. Fourth Edition. Royal 8vo, with Engravings, £1, 11s. 6d.

In preparing the present Edition, the Author has carefully re-written the book,
and added nearly one hundred new sections upon important subjects, which were
necessary to bring it up to the advanced state of the times, and to make it in all
respects worthy of continuing in public favour, as a complete directory in all matters
connected with the improved state of Arboriculture at the present day.

"What we have often stated in these columns we now repeat, that the book before us is the
most useful guide to good arboriculture in the English language."—*Review of Third Edition in
Gardeners' Chronicle by Dr Lindley.*

**Brown**—THE BOOK OF THE LANDED ESTATE.
By ROBERT E. BROWN, Factor and Estate Agent, Wass, Yorkshire.
Royal 8vo, with numerous Engravings, £1, 1s.

**Burbidge**—DOMESTIC FLORICULTURE, WINDOW GAR-
DENING, AND FLORAL DECORATIONS. By F. W. BURBIDGE.
Crown 8vo, with numerous Illustrations, 7s. 6d.

CONTENTS :—Gardening in the House.—Window Gardening.—Balcony Gar-
dening and Decoration.—Propagation of Plants—Soils, Potting, Watering, &c.—
Gardening in close Cases.—Wintering Tender Plants.—Hyacinths and other
Bulbs in Water and at Windows.—Orchids for Sitting-Rooms.—Bouquets, Vases,
and Wreaths.—Dinner-Table Decorations, and arranging of Fruits.—Drying
Flowers, Ferns, Grasses, &c.—Skeletonising Leaves, Seed-Vessels, &c.—De-
scriptive Lists of Suitable Flowering and Foliage Plants, Hardy Shrubs, &c.—
Exotic Plants for Warm and Sheltered Localities out of doors.—&c. &c. &c.

**Burn**—THE HANDBOOK OF THE MECHANICAL ARTS :
Being Practical Hints on the Construction and Arrangement of Dwellings
and other Buildings, and in Carpentry, Smith-Work, Cements, Plastering,
Brick-Making, Well-Sinking, Enclosing of Land, Road-Making, &c. By
R. SCOTT BURN, Engineer. In 8vo, with numerous Illustrations.
Second Edition, 6s. 6d.

**Burn**—PRACTICAL VENTILATION,

As applied to Public, Domestic, and Agricultural Structures ; with Remarks on Heating, Construction of Fire-Places, Cure of Smoky Chimneys, and an Appendix on the Ventilation of Ships, Steamboats, and Railway Carriages. By the SAME. Crown 8vo, 6s.

**Cruikshank**—THE PRACTICAL PLANTER :

Containing Directions for the Planting of Waste Land and Management of Wood, with a new method of Rearing the Oak. By THOMAS CRUIK-SHANK, Forester at Careston. 8vo, 12s.

**Dick** — OCCASIONAL PAPERS ON VETERINARY SUB-JECTS. By WILLIAM DICK, Late Professor of Veterinary Surgery to the Highland and Agricultural Society of Scotland, Veterinary Surgeon to the Queen for Scotland, Founder of the Edinburgh Veterinary College, &c. With a Portrait, and Memoir by R. O. PRINGLE. 8vo, 12s. 6d.

"The present work, which consists of gleanings from the elaborate opinions of Professor Dick on the numerous diseases to which horse and cattle flesh is heir, is a highly useful one. To the veterinary student it must prove an invaluable assistant, while it will go far to strengthen the hands of the experienced practitioner. A more thoroughly practical work we have seldom perused. Every subject is treated in a sound and sensible manner—the meanest capacity can understand the teaching of Professor Dick."—*Sportsman.*

**Galbraith** — TRIGONOMETRICAL SURVEYING, LEVEL-LING, AND RAILWAY ENGINEERING. By WILLIAM GAL-BRAITH, M.A. 8vo, 7s. 6d.

**THE GARDENER** :

A Magazine of Horticulture and Floriculture. Edited by DAVID THOMSON, Author of 'A Practical Treatise on the Culture of the Pine-Apple,' 'The Handy Book of the Flower Garden,' &c. ; Assisted by a Staff of the best practical writers. Published Monthly, 6d.

**Grieve**—ON ORNAMENTAL-FOLIAGED PELARGONIUMS ;

With Practical Hints for their Production, Propagation, and Cultivation. By PETER GRIEVE, Culford, Bury St Edmunds. Second Edition, enlarged, including description of Best Varieties introduced up to the present time, and Engravings. Crown 8vo, 4s.

**Harkness**—THE PREPARATION OF COOKED FOOD FOR THE FATTENING OF CATTLE, AND THE ADVANTAGE OF USING IT ALONG WITH CUT STRAW, HAY, TURNIPS, OR OTHER VEGETABLES. By THOMAS HARKNESS. 6d.

**Hole**—A BOOK ABOUT ROSES, *

How TO GROW AND SHOW THEM. ' By S. REYNOLDS HOLE, Author of 'A Little Tour in Ireland.' Fourth Edition, enlarged. Crown 8vo, 7s. 6d.

"It is the production of a man who boasts of thirty 'all England' cups, whose Roses are always looked for anxiously at flower-shows, who took the lion's share in originating the first Rose-show pur et simple, whose assistance as judge or amicus curiæ is always courted at such exhibitions, such a man 'ought to have something to say worth hearing to those who love the Rose,' and he has said it."—*Gardeners' Chronicle.*

"We cordially recommend the book to every amateur who wishes to grow Roses as at once the pleasantest and best yet written on the subject."—*The Field.*

**Hole**—THE SIX OF SPADES:
    A Book about the Garden and the Gardener. By the SAME. Crown 8vo, 5s.

    " We may, in conclusion, recommend the whole book to the attention of our readers as one which will afford them much amusement on a winter's night. . . . It is written by one who really loves flowers, and wishes to lead others to worship at the same shrine: and we wish the book success."—*Journal of Horticulture.*

**Johnston**—ELEMENTS OF AGRICULTURAL CHEMISTRY
    AND GEOLOGY. By JAMES F. W. JOHNSTON, F.R.S.E., F.G.S., &c. Ninth Edition, greatly enlarged. Revised and Edited by GEORGE T. ATKINSON, B.A., F.C.S., Clifton College, Bristol. 6s. 6d.

———— A CATECHISM OF AGRICULTURAL CHEMISTRY
    AND GEOLOGY. By the SAME. Revised by Dr AUGUSTUS VOELCKER, Consulting Chemist to the Royal Agricultural Society of England. Sixty-seventh thousand, with Engravings, 1s.

———— CONTRIBUTIONS TO SCIENTIFIC AGRICULTURE.
    By the SAME. Demy 8vo, 6s.

———— INSTRUCTIONS FOR THE ANALYSIS OF SOILS,
    LIMESTONES, AND MANURES. By the SAME. Fourth Edition, 2s.

———— ON THE USE OF LIME IN AGRICULTURE.
    By the SAME. Fcap. 8vo, 6s.

———— EXPERIMENTAL AGRICULTURE;
    Being the Results of Past, and Suggestions for Future Experiments in Scientific and Practical Agriculture. By the SAME. In 8vo, 8s.

**Johnstone**—ELKINGTON'S SYSTEM OF DRAINING.
    By J. JOHNSTONE. A New Edition. 4to, 10s. 6d.

JOURNAL OF AGRICULTURE,
    AND TRANSACTIONS OF THE HIGHLAND AND AGRICULTURAL SOCIETY OF SCOTLAND. Old Series, 1828 to 1843, 21 vols. bound in cloth, £3, 3s. New Series, 1843 to 1865, 22 vols. £4, 4s.

TRANSACTIONS OF THE HIGHLAND AND AGRICUL-
    TURAL SOCIETY OF SCOTLAND. 1866-1871, 6 Nos., sewed 4s. each : 1872-1874, cloth, 5s. each. Continued Annually.

**Laidlaw** — TABLES FOR CONVERTING LINLITHGOW
    BARLEY MEASURE INTO IMPERIAL BUSHELS AND STONES. Showing the value of one Lippie to eighty-one Bolls, at different rates per Bushel and Stone. Prepared by WILLIAM LAIDLAW, assistant to Charles Stewart, Esq, Hillside. Fcap. 8vo, 5s.

**M'Combie**—CATTLE AND CATTLE BREEDERS.
    By WILLIAM M'COMBIE, M.P., Tillyfour. A New and Cheaper Edition. 2s. 6d., cloth.

**Mackay** — ON THE MANAGEMENT OF LANDED PROPERTY IN THE HIGHLANDS OF SCOTLAND. By GEORGE C. MACKAY, C.E. Crown 8vo, 1s. 6d.

**M'Intosh** — THE BOOK OF THE GARDEN.

By CHARLES M'INTOSH, formerly Curator of the Royal Gardens of his Majesty the King of the Belgians, and lately of those of his Grace the Duke of Buccleuch, K.G., at Dalkeith Palace. In two large vols. royal 8vo, embellished with 1350 Engravings.

The work is divided into two great sections, each occupying a volume—the first comprising the formation, arrangement, and laying out of gardens, and the construction of garden buildings ; the second treating of the theory and practice of horticulture. Sold separately—viz. :

VOL. I. ON THE FORMATION OF GARDENS AND CONSTRUCTION OF GARDEN EDIFICES. 776 pages, and 1073 Engravings, £2, 10s.
VOL. II. PRACTICAL GARDENING. 868 pages, and 279 Engravings, £1, 17s. 6d.

**Mulder** — THE CHEMISTRY OF VEGETABLE AND ANIMAL PHYSIOLOGY. By DR J. G. MULDER. Professor of Chemistry in the University of Utrecht. Translated by Dr P. F. H. FROMBERG ; with an Introduction and Notes by Professor JOHNSTON. 22 coloured Plates, 8vo, £1, 10s.

**Pettigrew** — THE HANDY BOOK OF BEES,

AND THEIR PROFITABLE MANAGEMENT. By A. PETTIGREW, Rusholme, Manchester. Crown 8vo, 4s. 6d.

"The author of this volume is evidently a practical man, and knows a great deal more about bees and their habits than most of the bee-keepers in England ; indeed he may be said to be a very master in the art of bee mysteries."—*Bell's Life in London.*

**Rait** — THE RELATIVE VALUE OF ROUND AND SAWN TIMBER, SHOWN BY MEANS OF TABLES AND DIAGRAMS. By JAMES RAIT, Land-Steward at Castle Forbes. In large 8vo, bound in cloth, 8s.

**Scott** — DAIRY MANAGEMENT AND FEEDING OF MILCH-COWS ; Being the recorded Experience of MRS AGNES SCOTT, Winkston, Peebles. Third Edition, fcap., 1s.

**Seller** — PHYSIOLOGY AT THE FARM,

IN AID OF REARING AND FEEDING THE LIVE STOCK. By WILLIAM SELLER, M.D., F.R.S.E., Fellow of the Royal College of Physicians, Edinburgh, formerly Lecturer on Materia Medica and Dietetics; and HENRY STEPHENS, F.R.S.E., Author of the 'Book of the Farm,' &c. Post 8vo, with Engravings, 16s.

SHOOTER'S DIARY OR GAMEBOOK,

For recording the Quantity of Grouse Killed, and Time and Place, Number of Guns, Names of Parties, how disposed of, &c. Octavo, bound in red leather, 4s.

**Smith**—ITALIAN IRRIGATION :
A Report on the Agricultural Canals at Piedmont and Lombardy, addressed to the Hon. the Directors of the East India Company ; with an Appendix, containing a Sketch of the Irrigation System of Northern and Central India. By LIEUT.-COL. R. BAIRD SMITH, F.G.S., Captain Bengal Engineers. Second Edition. Two vols. 8vo, with Atlas in folio, 30s.

**Starforth**—VILLA RESIDENCES AND FARM ARCHITEC-TURE : A Series of Designs. By JOHN STARFORTH, Architect. 102 Engravings. Second Edition, medium 4to, £2, 17s. 6d.

—— VILLA RESIDENCES ;
A Series of Designs, with Descriptions. By the SAME. Forty Engravings. Medium quarto, 25s.

## THE STATISTICAL ACCOUNT OF SCOTLAND.

Complete with Index, 15 vols. 8vo, £16, 16s. Each County sold separately, with Title, Index, and Map, neatly bound in cloth, at the prices annexed, forming a very valuable Manual to the Landowner, the Tenant, the Manufacturer, the Naturalist, the Tourist, &c.

| | s. | d. | | s. | d. |
|---|---|---|---|---|---|
| Aberdeen | 25 | 0 | Kincardine | 8 | 0 |
| Argyll | 15 | 0 | Kinross | 2 | 6 |
| Ayr | 18 | 0 | Kirkcudbright | 8 | 6 |
| Banff | 9 | 0 | Lanark | 21 | 0 |
| Berwick | 8 | 6 | Linlithgow | 4 | 6 |
| Bute | 3 | 0 | Nairn | 1 | 6 |
| Caithness | 4 | 6 | Orkney | 5 | 6 |
| Clackmannan | 3 | 6 | Peebles | 4 | 6 |
| Dumbarton | 6 | 0 | Perth | 27 | 0 |
| Dumfries | 12 | 6 | Renfrew | 12 | 6 |
| Edinburgh | 16 | 6 | Ross and Cromarty | 10 | 6 |
| Elgin | 6 | 0 | Roxburgh | 10 | 6 |
| Fife | 21 | 0 | Selkirk | 2 | 6 |
| Forfar | 15 | 0 | Shetland | 4 | 6 |
| Haddington | 8 | 6 | Stirling | 10 | 0 |
| Inverness | 11 | 6 | Sutherland | 5 | 6 |
| | | | Wigtown | 5s. | 6d. |

**Stephens**—THE BOOK OF THE FARM,
Detailing the Labours of the Farmer, Farm-Steward, Ploughman, Shepherd, Hedger, Farm-Labourer, Field-Worker, and Cattleman. By HENRY STEPHENS, F.R.S.E. Illustrated with Portraits of Animals painted from the life ; and with 557 Engravings on Wood, representing the principal Field Operations, Implements, and Animals treated of in the Work. A New and Revised Edition, the third, in great part Rewritten. 2 vols. large 8vo, £2, 10s.

"From its first appearance a quarter of a century ago, until now, 'The Book of the Farm' has held the very highest rank as a book of reference on matters connected with the theory and practice of agriculture. . . . In the new edition before us the author has not been contented to put upon his ears, or trust the results of half-forgotten labours ; but from the mass of notes and criticisms with which he has in the interval kept his knowledge on support with the age, he has re-written page upon page and chapter after chapter, so that really 'The Book of the Farm' now before us is almost a new work. . . . We can unreservedly commend this new edition, and we should augur well for the agricultural future of this country if it could find a place on every farmer's bookshelf. It is in its favour that it contains within four covers all the book-learning a farmer need know."—*Saturday Review, 30th March 1872.*

**Stephens**—THE BOOK OF FARM IMPLEMENTS AND
MACHINES. By J. SLIGHT and R. SCOTT BURN, Engineers.
Edited by HENRY STEPHENS, F.R.S.E., Author of 'The Book of the
Farm,' &c. In 1 vol. large 8vo, uniform with 'The Book of the Farm,'
£2, 2s.

—— THE BOOK OF FARM-BUILDINGS;
Their Arrangement and Construction. By HENRY STEPHENS, F.R.S.E.,
Author of 'The Book of the Farm;' and ROBERT SCOTT BURN. Illustrated with 1045 Plates and Engravings. In 1 vol. large 8vo, uniform
with 'The Book of the Farm,' &c. £1, 11s. 6d.

—— YESTER DEEP LAND-CULTURE;
Being a Detailed Account of the Method of Cultivation which has been suc-
cessfully practised for several years by the Marquess of Tweeddale at Yester.
By HENRY STEPHENS, F.R.S.E., Author of 'The Book of the Farm.'
In fcap. 8vo, 4s. 6d.

The characteristic of the new system—for it may be well so named, different as it
is from any now in use—is the complete pulverisation of the subsoil, and its mixture
with the upper soil, the treatment being of a very substantial and permanent nature.

—— PRACTICAL SYSTEM OF FARM BOOK-KEEPING;
Being that recommended in the 'Book of the Farm' by H. Stephens.
Royal Octavo, 2s. 6d.
Also, SEVEN FOLIO ACCOUNT BOOKS, printed and ruled in accord-
ance with the System, the whole being especially adapted for keeping, by
an easy and accurate method, an account of all the transactions of the
Farm. A detailed Prospectus may be had from the publishers. Price of
the complete set of Eight Books, £1, 7s. Also, A LABOUR AC-
COUNT OF THE ESTATE, 2s. 6d.

—— A MANUAL OF PRACTICAL DRAINING.
By the SAME. Third Edition, 8vo, 5s.

—— CATECHISM OF PRACTICAL AGRICULTURE.
By the SAME, with Engravings. 1s.

**Steuart**—THE PLANTER'S GUIDE.
By SIR HENRY STEUART, BART. of Allanton. To which is prefixed a
Biographical Sketch of the Author, and an Engraving from a Portrait by Rae-
burn. A New Edition, with the Author's last Additions and Corrections,
8vo, 21s.

**Stuart**—AGRICULTURAL LABOURERS,
AS THEY WERE, ARE, AND SHOULD BE, IN THEIR SOCIAL CONDITION.
By the REV. HARRY STUART, A.M., Minister of Oathlaw. 8vo,
Second Edition, 1s.

**Sutherland** — HAND BOOK OF HARDY HERBACEOUS
AND ALPINE FLOWERS, FOR GENERAL GARDEN DECORATION.
Containing Descriptions, in Plain Language, of upwards of 1000 Species of
Ornamental Hardy Perennial and Alpine Plants, adapted to all classes of
Flower-Gardens, Rockwork, and Waters ; along with Concise and Plain
Instructions for their Propagation and Culture. By WILLIAM SUTHER-
LAND, Gardener to the Earl of Minto ; formerly Manager of the Her-
baceous Department at Kew. Crown 8vo, 7s. 6d.

" This is an unpretending but valuable work, well adapted to furnish information respecting
a class of plants certainly rising in popular estimation. . . . We cordially recommend his
book to the notice of our readers, as likely to be, from a gardening point of view, the standard
work on Herbaceous Plants."—*Gardeners' Chronicle.*
" The best book of its class available for English readers."—*Gardener's Magazine.*

**Thomson**—HANDY BOOK OF THE FLOWER-GARDEN :
Being Practical Directions for the Propagation, Culture, and Arrangement
of Plants in Flower-Gardens all the year round. Embracing all classes of
Gardens, from the largest to the smallest. With Engraved and Coloured
Plans, illustrative of the various systems of Grouping in Beds and Borders.
By DAVID THOMSON, Gardener to his Grace the Duke of Buccleuch,
K.G., at Drumlanrig. A New and Enlarged Edition, crown 8vo, 7s. 6d.

" Its author is entitled to great praise for the simple and clear manner in which he has explained
the cultural directions, which, if carefully complied with, will enable the non-professional floricul-
turist to grow plants as well as any gardener."—*Gardeners' Chronicle.*

———— THE HANDY BOOK OF FRUIT CULTURE UNDER
GLASS. Being a series of Elaborate Practical Treatises on the cultivation
and forcing of Pines, Vines, Peaches, Figs, Melons, Strawberries, and Cucum-
bers. With Engravings of hothouses, &c., most suitable for the cultivation
and forcing of these fruits. By the SAME. In crown 8vo, with Engravings, 7s. 6d.

" The author is well known to be a thorough master of his profession, and one of the most able
and best practical gardeners of the present day. We therefore expected, on opening this volume,
to find it brimful of good sound practical advice, and we have not been disappointed. The work
before us is a true gardener's book."—*Gardeners' Chronicle.*

**Thomson**—A PRACTICAL TREATISE ON THE CULTIVA-
TION OF THE GRAPE VINE. By WILLIAM THOMSON, for-
merly Gardener to his Grace the Duke of Buccleuch, K.G., Dalkeith Park.
Seventh Edition, Enlarged, 8vo, 5s.

" We cannot too strongly recommend Mr Thomson's treatise as a thoroughly practical and sure
guide to the cultivation of the vine."—*Journal of Horticulture.*
" We urge our readers to procure the work, and they will get so clear an insight into vine grow-
ing that a vinery will become one of the necessaries of existence."—*Field.*

www.ingramcontent.com/pod-product-compliance
Lightning Source LLC
Chambersburg PA
CBHW031757090426
42739CB00008B/1049